THE CHINA

BREAKTHROUGH

THE CHINA BREAKTHROUGH

Whitlam in the Middle Kingdom, 1971

BILLY GRIFFITHS

 MONASH University Publishing

Monash University Publishing
Building 4, Monash University
Clayton, Victoria 3800, Australia
www.publishing.monash.edu
www.publishing.monash.edu/books/cb-9781921867644.html

Monash University Publishing brings to the world publications which advance the best traditions of humane and enlightened thought. Monash University Publishing titles pass through a rigorous process of independent peer review.

Design: Les Thomas

Cover image: Gough Whitlam on the Great Wall of China, July 1971. Reproduced courtesy of Newspix/News Ltd.

National Library of Australia Cataloguing-in-Publication entry:

Author: Griffiths, Billy.

Title: The China Breakthrough: Whitlam in the Middle Kingdom, 1971/ Billy Griffiths.

ISBN: 9781921867644 (pbk.)

Series: Australian history.

Notes: Includes bibliographical references and index.

Subjects: Whitlam, Gough, 1916-; China--Foreign relations--1949-1976; China--Foreign relations--1976-; Australia--Foreign relations--United States; China--Foreign relations--Australia; Australia--Foreign relations-- United States; United States--Foreign relations--Australia.

Dewey Number: 327.9405109045

Printed in Australia by Griffin Press an Accredited ISO AS/NZS 14001:2004 Environmental Management System printer.

The paper this book is printed on is certified by the Programme for the Endorsement of Forest Certification scheme. Griffin Press holds PEFC chain of custody SGS - PEFC/COC-0594. PEFC promotes environmentally responsible, socially beneficial and economically viable management of the world's forests.

For

M.E.R.

&

E.G.M.

'You have had many barbarian invasions, but I am not sure that you are prepared for this one.'

Henry Kissinger, US Assistant for National Security Affairs, to Chinese Premier Zhou Enlai, Peking, 11 July 1971 (Gough Whitlam's 55th Birthday).

Foreword

Three of the six-member Whitlam delegation to China in mid-1971 wrote accounts of that event, immediately afterwards and in the next few years: Whitlam himself, Graham Freudenberg, that gifted and most famous of speech-writers in Australia's political history, and myself. Several of the accompanying press party, including Ross Terrill who was then an academic at Harvard, also wrote retrospective accounts. So much has been written since that it might seem there is nothing more to say. But this book by Billy Griffiths is fresh, enlivened by an intelligent assembly of what seems to be all the available information, full of new insights, and vivid in its reconstruction of this formative event which inaugurated a fundamental change in the way Australia relates to Asia. Appearing in a year when Australia is marking the fortieth anniversary of diplomatic relations, his study brings back into focus the real beginning of the relationship with China – and its antecedent, Gough Whitlam's calling for recognition of the communist government in Beijing from the time of his first speech after election to the federal parliament in 1954. His was a considered, not an expedient or opportunistic position. It was founded on a rational approach to international affairs and a principle of independence in foreign policy, even within an alliance with the United States. So when he went to China as Opposition Leader in 1971, before we had official relations, this was consistent with his approach and his principle, but it was not without political risk to him and his party. Attacking China and those who dealt with it had been an effective leitmotif in the policies of the conservative government in power since the early 1950s – and for most of the media, as well as for the nation's anti-communists, xenophobes and racists. Whitlam's decision was courageous. But it was not quixotic.

He knew very clearly what he was doing. He would have made the decision on his principled stand, but he had also read the portents of change better than any of his detractors. Griffiths gives us the best and most forensic account to date of what ensued, and an eminently readable one at that.

Despite its serious purpose and the weight of political consequences for Whitlam and his colleagues, there was an almost light-headed quality to the mood of that delegation. This was not intoxication with China, although venturing into that unknown, sequestered and forbidden world provided its own excitement. It was, rather, a sense of liberation from the constraints of opposition, a striking out from the thinking of the ruling conservative parties which had dominated Australian foreign policy for twenty-one years, into international diplomacy on behalf of Australia. It was a foretaste of government. After the meeting with Premier Zhou Enlai in the Great Hall of the People, which sealed a high-level agreement on the terms of diplomatic relations, Whitlam's mood was one not of triumphalism but of fulfilment, a deep sense of satisfaction that he had now, in effect, already implemented a key policy of his yet-to-be elected government. It was indeed a bizarre and heady moment in Australia's diplomatic history, with Henry Kissinger next in line to meet Premier Zhou in that same Great Hall only a few days later and, sadly, the McMahon government at home beating an anti-China drum and proclaiming 'China has been a political asset to the Liberal Party in the past and is likely to remain one in the future.'

There is nothing in Australian history to compare with that change in Australia's international posture. It was not a changing of a policy by a government, a cabinet sitting together to deliberate, a sending of an official delegate, a cabling of instructions to an ambassador to get in touch with a Chinese counterpart in a third country. It was a personal commitment to the fray, from opposition not from government, an expedition, of great bravado and exposure, but great political judgement and luck. It was a journey to the unknown because none of us really knew what if anything would come of it or even who Whitlam would meet. It was personal diplomacy of great sensitivity on many counts.

And it became a foreign policy executed from opposition. After the ALP's announcement that it had sought an invitation to visit China to discuss Australia-China relations, and before we set off for Beijing, the McMahon government had finally accepted what was happening globally with China and rushed to announce that it would recognise Beijing, although it stumbled around with unworkable terms and conditions for eighteen months, until its defeat at the 1972 election. But it had in fact surrendered its long-held position and committed to the same objective as the ALP, even if it tied itself in knots trying to achieve this with a Two-Chinas policy. Whitlam had made a pre-emptive move, and by this effectively committed Australia to changing a China policy that had been in place for two decades. As a political finesse, it was a work of art.

It was not just about our relations with China; it was more broadly, and deeply, about Asia. Vietnam had been the catalyst for the first major shift in public attitudes to Asia since Federation, by getting Australians to acknowledge that it was there. Breaking the political embargo on relations with China was the central and symbolic beginning of Australia's coming to terms with that Asia. It was Whitlam's achievement. I am glad to have been there.

—*Stephen FitzGerald, 2 June 2012*

Contents

Acknowledgements

In mostly unconscious ways, many environments have influenced the perspectives of this book. Travels to Beijing, Shanghai, Nanjing and Wuxi helped me to ground the abstractions of diplomatic documents in contemporary experience and the natural world. More locally, I reflect on the study environments afforded to me by friends and family in Carlton, O'Connor, Bar Point, Chippendale and Glebe, where many of the ideas in this book were generated. I am grateful to all who have helped and supported me over the course of the research and writing.

To Steve FitzGerald I owe a great debt. I thank him for his insights and recollections. It has been an honour to talk and work with someone who has been so influential in shaping the international relationship at the heart of this book.

Special thanks are due to the conscientious and endlessly obliging librarians and archivists at the National Archives of Australia (Canberra and Sydney offices) and the National Library of Australia for their help seeking security clearances, arranging the use of oral histories and special collections, and generally arguing my case in all research matters. I am also grateful to all those at the Whitlam Institute, Fisher Library, Mitchell Library , National Museum of Australia Library and the State Library of Victoria, who, wittingly and unwittingly, have contributed to this work.

Several people with whom I spoke only briefly about this project were nevertheless instrumental in helping me clarify my ideas and intentions. I especially wish to thank for that reason Bain Attwood, Jocelyn Chey, John Hirst, Julia Kindt, Neville Meaney and the late Jamie Mackie. For their invaluable help with the logistics of my research, I thank Jane Brown, Peter Brown, Ian Davies and Ian Maxwell. For his wit, wisdom, and editing brilliance, I thank

Fraser Raeburn. I am also indebted to four anonymous referees for their thoughtful and constructive comments on this book in manuscript form.

Many of the ideas in this book first saw the light of day at a forum organised by Historians of Australia's Foreign Relations at the ANU in November 2011. I am grateful to those who made that event possible and to all who offered me feedback and encouragement.

I feel very fortunate to have worked with Nathan Hollier, Jo Mullins and the talented team at Monash University Publishing. I thank them for their hard work and good humour, and for making the publishing experience a wholly positive one.

My family has made writing this book a pleasure. I thank my parents, Tom and Libby, and my sister Kate, for their constant enthusiasm and support. This book is dedicated to my Grannie, Elizabeth Robin, who established my family's link with China; and to my partner, Emily Morrice, without whose love and support this book could not have been written.

And last, but certainly not least, I owe a great debt to James Curran. I thank him for his advice, assistance, criticism and encouragement.

—*Billy Griffiths*

Chinese in the Text

Although the older 'post-office' romanisation was current throughout the period under study, I have transliterated the Chinese in this text in the modern *pinyin* way. Hence Mao Tse-tung (毛泽东) appears as Mao Zedong. I have kept the older system of transliteration only for place names. I use, for example, Peking, not Beijing. In doing this I hope to preserve some of the historical weight these names carry. Peking represents a city of the past; Beijing evokes the modern day capital. For consistency I have extended my chosen transliteration to in-text quotes. I list below the transliterations which I use in the text and their variations.

Post Office	Pinyin
Peking	Beijing
Chungking	Chongqing
Canton	Guangzhou
Nanking	Nanjing
Shumchun	Shenzhen
Taipei	Taibei
Yangtze	Yangzi
Mao Tse-tung	Mao Zedong
Chou En-lai	Zhou Enlai
Chiang Kai-shek	Jiang Jieshi
Chi Peng-fei	Ji Pengfei
Pai Hsiang-kuo	Bai Xiangguo
Teng Hsiao-ping	Deng Xiaoping

A note on 'Middle Kingdom'

China is called 'Zhongguo' in Mandarin Chinese. The first character, *zhong*, means 'central' or 'middle', while *guo* is variously translated as 'state', 'states', 'nation', or 'kingdom'. For generations, those who came from outside Chinese borders, who travelled to the Middle Kingdom from across the wide sea, were regarded as *yemanren*: foreigners, wild men, barbarians.[1]

List of Illustrations

Front cover image

Gough Whitlam on the Great Wall of China, July 1971 (Newspix/ News Limited)

Introduction

The ALP delegation on the Great Wall of China, July 1971, (from left) Mick Young, Tom Burns, Stephen FitzGerald, Gough Whitlam, Rex Patterson and Graham Freudenberg (Newspix/ News Limited)

The accompanying journalists on the Great Wall of China, July 1971, (from left) Derek McKendry (ABC Cameraman), John Stubbs (SMH), Willie Phua (ABC Soundman), Kenneth Randall (The Australian), Eric Walsh (News Ltd), Philip Koch (ABC Correspondent), Allan Barnes (The Age), Laurie Oakes (Herald and Weekly Times) and David Barnett (AAP) (Photograph courtesy of Stephen FitzGerald)

Chapter One

Australian students about to tour China study a large wall map of Asia, 1957 (National Archives of Australia/W. Bundle: A1501, A904/1)

Chapter Two

Whitlam talks with Zhou Enlai in the Great Hall of the People, 5 July 1971 (National Archives of Australia: M155, B22)

Henry Kissinger shakes Zhou Enlai's hand, 9 July 1971 (Associated Press)

Chapter Three

American President Richard Nixon escorts Australian Prime Minister William McMahon from the White House, Washington DC, 2 November 1971 (Bettmann/CORBIS)

Gough Whitlam speaking to journalists upon returning from his visit to China, July 1971 (National Library of Australia, an2970638)

Epilogue

Gough Whitlam listens at the Echo Wall in the Temple of Heaven in Peking, November 1973 (National Archives of Australia: A6180, 14/11/73/209)

The ALP delegation on the Great Wall of China, July 1971
From left: Mick Young, Tom Burns, Stephen FitzGerald, Gough Whitlam, Rex
Patterson and Graham Freudenberg.

The accompanying journalists on the Great Wall of China, July 1971

From left: Derek McKendry (ABC Cameraman), John Stubbs (SMH), Willie Phua (ABC Soundman), Kenneth Randall (The Australian), Eric Walsh (News Ltd), Philip Koch (ABC Correspondent), Allan Barnes (The Age), Laurie Oakes (Herald and Weekly Times) and David Barnett (AAP).

Photo courtesy of Stephen FitzGerald

Introduction

On 2 December 1972, the Australian Labor Party came to power after twenty-three years in Opposition. The swing towards Labor had been relatively small: 2.5 per cent. But it was enough. It gave the new government a nine-seat majority and the new Prime Minister, Gough Whitlam, a mandate for change. Governing as a duumvirate with Lance Barnard, Whitlam enacted reform at an unprecedented pace. Within weeks, his Government had extended political recognition to the People's Republic of China, ended conscription, destroyed the last vestiges of White Australia, supported equal pay for women, begun reform of the health service, abolished British honours and started the search for a new national anthem. Political commentators had difficulty keeping up with it all; *The Sydney Morning Herald* and *The Age* started columns on their front pages listing 'What the Government did today'.[1]

Whitlam's campaign video, engineered by Labor Federal Secretary Mick Young, has become somewhat iconic of the heady mood of the early 1970s. It featured an exuberant chorus of Australian personalities singing and grooving, while a sequence of images – of Whitlam as a boy, as a husband, and as a statesman – flashed with increasing frequency to the climactic catch-phrase: 'It's Time!' One of the images in the jingle is of Whitlam shaking hands with the Premier of the People's Republic of China, Zhou Enlai. The photo was taken in July 1971 when Whitlam, as Opposition Leader, travelled to China with a small party of Australians. His mission: to foster friendly relations with an important foreign power, find a resolution to a trade issue, and exploit the tattered nature of the Australian Government's China policy.

The visit, as this book explores, was a defining event in Australia's cultural, political and diplomatic reorientation towards Asia. It was also a moment of theatre. A matter of days after Whitlam shook Zhou's hand, the US President's envoy, Henry Kissinger, secretly engaged in the same diplomatic ritual. Whitlam had the good fortune to find himself at the epicentre of a seismic shift in America-China relations. The coincidence, in the words of Bill Hayden, recast 'a disaster in the making' into 'a stroke of genius'.[2] It transformed Whitlam's image as a statesman and gave his candidacy for the Prime Ministership renewed momentum. But the Kissinger visit, however beneficial it was for Whitlam politically, also tends to overshadow the substance of Whitlam's visit. What was a bold piece of foreign policy in its own right – an irresistible vignette of Whitlam's time in office – has become remembered primarily as a case of fortuitous timing, or as a 'photo opportunity that placed Whitlam firmly on the world stage'.[3] This book tries to refocus the historical lens on Whitlam's 1971 China initiative: to explore the importance of the overlapping American and Australian visits, but also to understand why Whitlam sought to go to China, what this meant in the Australian context, and why his visit created such controversy.

✴

The impact of Whitlam's trip to China in 1971 continues to reverberate today, especially amongst members of the ALP. In 2010, Prime Minister Kevin Rudd spoke fondly of the visit. He remembered sitting in front of the television in 1971 and watching broadcasts of the delegation in China. Mesmerised by the images, he yearned to learn more of Chinese culture and was left with a deep impression of Labor's role in world affairs. The visit spurred him to study Chinese history and language at university. Later he would serve as a diplomat in China and, in 2007, he became the first Western leader to speak fluent Mandarin. As journalist David Marr writes of Rudd,

> That single event still illuminates his political imagination. Forty years later, as I'm walking along the beach in Mackay with him, he exclaims: 'What leadership!'[4]

Rudd's reaction is important to understanding the two driving themes behind this book. First, Rudd's experience reveals perhaps the most profound influence of the visit. Through the travels of Australians such as Whitlam, who led arguably the most politically significant and widely publicised visit since the formation of the PRC in 1949, China gradually lost its fantastical and forbidding image. That Kevin Rudd, as an Australian thirteen year-old, was excited and absorbed by an Asian culture is revealing of the new role China was assuming in at least some Australians' imagination.

The other important aspect of Rudd's reflection is his vagueness about the whole affair. To David Marr in 2010, he recalled the 1971 visit as particularly influential. Elsewhere, he reflects that it was the 1973 visit of Gough and Margaret Whitlam to China that sparked his interest in Chinese culture.[5] At first glance, the mix-up of dates seems immaterial: the product of a busy man's hazy childhood memory. But, with close attention to the literature of this period, it is striking how often Rudd's mistake has been repeated. Despite the familiarity many Australians have with this moment, surprisingly little is actually known of the enterprise. Whitlam's visit to China has become a stopping point on the way to another argument, an anecdotal flourish to a discussion of Sino-Australian diplomacy, or a footnote to Whitlam's career. It is usually passed over in fleeting reference, explained away in a sentence or, at most, granted a few pages of analysis in a volume

xxiv | *The China Breakthrough*

of larger scope.[6] Never has Whitlam's visit been singled out by an impartial historian and viewed on its own merits. Perhaps it is for this reason that the visit becomes blurred with other events, and that when it is explored, the account is more often than not tarnished by factual errors.[7] This book is a concerted effort to reclaim the narrative of the ALP delegation to China in 1971: to tell a story that has implications far beyond political image and contingent circumstances. The 1971 visit marked the end of Australian thinking about China in terms of red and yellow threats; it was a crucial cultural encounter in a new phase of Australian engagement with Asia; and, ultimately, it exposed the fragmented nature of Australian foreign policy in a post-imperial and increasingly multi-polar world.

A note on the sources

The frequency with which errors are reproduced about this visit can be explained to some extent by its unofficial nature. Whitlam was in Opposition in 1971, and the visit was made at private expense; thus the records have not been archived as thoroughly as would an official visit by a Prime Minister. Simple facts such as the delegation's itinerary, transcripts of the meetings in Peking, and even who was involved, are not easy to find.[8] Yet, given the rich array of published primary sources, it is astounding that the wider implications of this visit are rarely drawn out.[9]

Stephen FitzGerald, Ross Terrill, Graham Freudenberg and Laurie Oakes, all of whom travelled with Whitlam in China in 1971, provide invaluable narratives of the event. FitzGerald is the lone scholar who has devoted a short book to the visit: *Talking with China*, published before the election in 1972.[10] It is a critical assessment of the contemporary state of Australian foreign policy and an impressive estimation of the prospects of an Australian diplomatic relationship with China. Terrill's book, *800,000,000: The Real China*, from which I borrow two of my chapter titles, also provides precious insight into the Australian visit, although it is primarily oriented towards familiarising American audiences with the idea of China.[11] Freudenberg and Oakes, both at the time and since, have written gracefully of the visit, although always with the political implications it had for Gough Whitlam at the forefront of their minds.[12] The other major historian of the event is, of course, Gough Whitlam, who does not shy away from reminding his audiences who sowed the seeds of Australia and China's diplomatic relationship.[13]

A comment on structure and style

In style, this book purposefully goes against the tempo of the current literature on this period. In order to clarify my approach I call upon words of the eminent British philosopher and historian, R.G. Collingwood, who once defined political history as the history of political thought:

> Consider how the historian describes a famous speech. He does not concern himself with any sensuous elements in it such as the pitch of the statesman's voice, the hardness of the benches, the deafness of the old gentleman in the third row; he concentrates his attention on what the man was trying to say (the thought, that is, expressed in words) and how his audience received it (the thoughts in their minds, and how these conditioned the impact upon them of the statesman's thought).[14]

This book is an argument for the place of hard benches in Australian political history. Words, statements and actions are, of course, the historian's central insight into the intentions of political actors and the reactions they inspire. But, for a thirteen year-old Kevin Rudd, like so many others, it was not words, but the sensuous elements of Whitlam's visit that captured his imagination. It was the flickering images of an Australian statesman politicking against the backdrop of an unfamiliar and fascinating country. It was the fact that Whitlam was talking about Australia and China's future from the train station at Lo Wu, sweating, with his jacket over his arm, as he was about to cross the border into China for the first time.[15] It was the sense that the ALP delegation was being politically adventurous, that they were striding into the unknown, and that the visit had dramatic and far-reaching political, diplomatic and cultural implications.

In order to capture the sensuous elements of the visit to China, I give time and space to the narrative with the belief that storytelling engenders its own insights. This approach complements the work of historians such as Edmund S.K. Fung, Roderic Pitty and Neville Meaney, who have each written superb analytical accounts of the visit on their way to making a broader argument about, respectively, the Australian Government's China policy in 1971–72, the problems of secret diplomacy, and Australia's changing alliance with America from 1971–75.[16] I draw out their arguments, as well as those of other relevant historians, in context throughout the course of the following chapters.

This book calls for the 1971 visit to China to be recognised as a pivotal moment not just for the Australian Labor Party, but also in Australia's relationship with China, its alliance with America, and its cultural and economic reorientation towards Asia. The argument falls into three parts. The first chapter explores how China has figured in the Australian imagination and Australian foreign policy since diplomatic ties were established with nationalist China in 1941. In the second chapter I unpack the theatre of the 1971 visit and deepen its political intrigue. The third chapter explores the immediate and lasting impacts of the visit. An epilogue offers a reflection on the significance of the visit for Sino-Australian relations through the story of imprisoned journalist Francis James.

Australian students about to tour China study a large wall map of Asia, 1957

National Archives of Australia

Chapter One

The Shimmering Mirage

China in the Australian imagination and

in Australian foreign policy

Shimmering mirage, a China conjured in our minds by scraps of news and speculation. Devilishly well organized; neat and regimented; striding ahead to overtake Russia and America; clean, abstemious; an army of sexless puppets, their daily life an incarnation of the Thought of Mao Zedong. Absence from China feeds the mirage. Fear, buttressed by ignorance, hints that China is formidable, or awful, or awfully formidable. How cunning those Chinese are! Do they not constantly surprise us? Such sacrifice of indulgence today for glory tomorrow!

Ross Terrill, *800,000,000: The Real China*, 1972[1]

Our story begins on Sunday 27 June 1971.[2] A Qantas aircraft flies low, weaving between sharp mountains shrouded in thick smog. It tips to the side in one final turn before straightening up and touching ground at Hong Kong airport. The air is heavy with moisture and the heat is a shock to the small group of Australians that disembark the plane. Months of preparation, political posturing and nervous anticipation have led to this point. And still they are not at their final destination. There is an air of excitement amongst the Australians, but also an intimation of the unknown. The dénouement of this visit is yet to be decided. They know neither where they will go once they cross the narrow channel of water to the territories of mainland China nor how they will be received when they get there.[3] Even those who have entered China before are unsure of what to expect in the coming days, what ravages the Cultural Revolution has wrought. The uncertainty plays on the mind of Gough Whitlam, the head of the delegation and leader of the Australian Labor Party; this visit could make or break his political career. His apprehension, however, is outweighed by a powerful sense of purpose. With this trip, he is putting a long-held policy into action. He has initiated what will be the first significant political contact between Australia and China for twenty-two years.

Places in the delegation had been hotly contested. The travelling members of the Australian Labor Party were not confirmed until that very morning at Sydney airport.[4] Of the sixty-eight journalists that applied to the Chinese Government to cover the visit, only nine would be granted visas.[5] The Australians are greeted at the airport and escorted to the Ambassador Hotel nearby.[6] The People's Republic of China, for so long relegated to abstraction – the subject of heated debate, charged imagination and Cold War paranoia – begins to assume a physical presence in the Australian minds. For five days they will wait in Hong Kong, gazing at the shimmering mirage on the horizon: forbidden, mysterious and rich with political possibility.

On 1 October 1949, after three years of political upheaval, the Chinese nationalists fell from power in mainland China and the People's Republic of China (PRC) was proclaimed. While Jiang Jieshi fled to Taiwan, the new communist government, led by Mao Zedong, declared its intention to establish diplomatic relations with friendly states. A new question came to dominate public debate across the globe: should the world recognise and thus legitimise this new government as the sole government of China?

In Australia, it seemed like a simple question. The Government felt no strong loyalty towards the exiled nationalists, Britain was making positive murmurings about effecting immediate recognition of the PRC, and China, through shared geography and sheer size, was of vital strategic importance to Australia. Recognition appeared inevitable. The Australian Embassy in nationalist China had already set about relocating to Peking. In November 1949, a conference was held in Canberra to discuss, amongst other things, the legitimacy of the new communist government. The outcome was a unanimous recommendation for Australia to adopt the policy of Britain.[7] On 6 January 1950 Britain recognised the PRC.[8] More than two decades would pass before Australia did the same.

How are we to interpret this delay? Why was recognition still a burning issue in 1971 when Opposition Leader Gough Whitlam travelled with a small delegation of Australians to China?

This chapter will explore these questions by probing the under-currents and continuities in Australia's attitude and policy towards China, mapping the progression from apathy to ambivalence and finally to hostility. It takes us first to nationalist China to examine the roots of Australia's diplomatic relations with China. It then reflects on the mental tapestry that shaped Australia-China relations in the 1950s and 60s. Finally, it explores how China lurched back into Australian political consciousness through a rapid succession of international events involving wheat, ping-pong and the Australian Labor Party.

I

'Like dealing with an echoing void'[9]

Late at night on 20 October 1941, a small plane flew into the wartime capital of nationalist China, Chungking. The engines roared as the aircraft touched down on a runway in the middle of the mighty Yangtze River. After hours of darkness the city lights were a friendly sight to one passenger on board; Sir Frederic Eggleston, Australia's first Minister Plenipotentiary to China, was peering through the small windows at his new home.

Less than six months earlier, in the back of a taxi outside the Treasury Gardens in Melbourne, Eggleston had been offered this position by the Minister for External Affairs, Sir Frederick Stewart.[10] It was a choice that acknowledged Eggleston's long campaign for 'pacific consciousness' in Australia.[11] It even seemed to vindicate his 1922 piece of strategic analysis: 'The policy of Australia is linked with the case of China'. But as Eggleston settled into his new role in Chungking he realised that his posting had not changed Australian attitudes. Australia was still very much a part of the British world and the Australian Government wanted above all to keep Asia and Asians at arm's length. China was a long way from the hearth of Empire, and, at this time, was not considered to be a part of Australia's destiny.

It was not until 1940 that the Australian Government had begun to establish its first overseas diplomatic missions outside of London. It was a reluctant act, a resignation that Britain and Australia – however closely bound by history, culture, and blood – could not act as one Empire: they had different geopolitical interests.[12] Eggleston's appointment to nationalist China was the third such post, after the strategically significant embassies in the United States and Japan. The opportunities presented by the new Department of External Affairs excited the Australian Prime Minister, Robert

Menzies. He judged Washington so important a post that he even considered taking it for himself. He was less enthusiastic to foster diplomatic relations with China. Keith Waller, who flew in with Eggleston that dark October night, explains that the decision to establish an Australian Embassy in Chunking was made 'partly to balance the fact that [Australia] had just opened one in Tokyo, and partly to show some support for the Chinese Government', who were at war with the Japanese.[13] It was a decision based on practicalities more than any aspirations to build a bridge between the two cultures.

Although he was severely handicapped by arthritis and gout, Eggleston had an agile mind and quickly became a prominent character in Chungking society. He mixed with local artists, writers and intellectuals, lectured at the universities, and attended exhibitions and the theatre. With the help of a translator and the British and American intelligence channels, he prided himself on running the best informed diplomatic mission in Chungking. He met often with the Generalissimo Jiang Jieshi and had brief but friendly relations with the liaison officer from the Communist Party, Zhou Enlai. Yet, as biographer Warren G. Osmond writes, 'Eggleston was virtually Australia's only form of intellectual or cultural exchange with China during the war, although this was due to his personal enthusiasm rather than official policy.'[14] The little contact that the two countries did have, through the United Nations aid scheme and in debate over Australia's immigration policy, riled the Australian Government. Jiang Jieshi's nationalist regime was openly criticised as being corrupt, incompetent and destined to collapse.[15]

After a year the legation moved to a new house in a poorer area of the city, alive with the chattering of ducks and the bustle of people in the narrow streets. The change of scene brought Eggleston to muse, 'I suppose now we are in the real China.'[16] This 'real China' was a far cry from the images that dominated the Australian Parliament and press. Whenever Eggleston read the Australian newspapers in Chungking, he became depressed and outraged at their lack of sophisticated analysis of international affairs, and of China especially. As Richard White reminds us, Australian images of China at this time belonged to a variety of Western Orientalism: scraps of information gleaned from 'school geography and history lessons, popular cultural figures such as Fu Manchu, penny dreadfuls, Hollywood blockbusters' and the like.[17] Very few Australians could relate to Eggleston's experience of 'being there'. In the absence of first-hand knowledge, wild stereotypes flourished.[18]

Eggleston felt frustrated and ignored in his new posting. Few letters arrived from home and most of his attempts to establish connections between the two countries fell on deaf ears. Even after Singapore succumbed to Japan in 1942 and Australia and China found themselves openly sharing a common enemy, Eggleston was not asked to use the powers of his post and pursue any substantial dealings with the Chinese. In the diary entries he sent back to the Department of External Affairs, he despaired at his isolation:

> I feel like children in the market-place – I pipe into you and you do not sing. Is it right to waste my sweetness on the desert air, in the vacant spaces of Australian minds?[19]

The neglect that Eggleston experienced is indicative of a deeper pattern in Australian relations with China. As one writer characterised it in 1943, Australia's attitude towards China was marked by an 'apathy that has neither feeling nor deliberate aloofness but merely the insular preoccupation of a people mostly interested in themselves and in those like them.'[20] Despite being in the same quarter of the globe, China was seen as distinctively 'other': foreign, fantastical and, in Eggleston's words, 'outside civilisation as we know it'.[21] Civilisation, as Australians knew it, was British. The sheer difference of China – in culture, language and race – bred in Australia an anxiety about the unknown, a fear of the unfamiliar.[22] It translated into a reluctance to engage with the mysterious Asian power to the near north. Of course, Australia's relationship with China has roots far deeper than the 1940s, but Eggleston's experience in nationalist China highlights that even before the communist government took power, and before the Cold War mentality locked down on the Western world, Australians regarded China with wariness, suspicion and anxiety.

An ambivalent relationship

This attitude changed with the inauguration of the People's Republic of China. Australia could no longer refrain from engagement; it was forced into a decision on the question of recognition. Apathy became replaced by ambivalence.[23] Although deputy Labor leader H.V. Evatt audaciously claimed in October 1949 that Australia, Britain, and the US had arranged to harmonise their approach to the PRC, Australia's two main allies were adopting contradictory policies.[24] Britain was tentatively endorsing early recognition while America was calling for Western countries and the United Nations to delay action as a stance against international communism. Australia's traditional ties to Britain directly clashed with its strategically significant friendship with the United States. The resulting course of inaction on China policy is but one sign of a shift in thinking in Australia's 'great and powerful friends'. Britain, although very much the cultural heart of Australia, was gradually receding as a foreign policy priority.

It is often forgotten that in 1949 and early 1950, Australia, under both Labor and Liberal leadership, seriously considered effecting immediate recognition of the newly proclaimed People's Republic of China. Labor Prime Minister Ben Chifley deemed early recognition of the PRC a judicious move, but for political reasons he postponed any action until after the federal election in December 1949. He was being assailed by the Opposition at the time for supposedly taking a soft line on communism, a claim that would surely gain force if he recognised the largest communist power in the world. A similar situation was being played out in New Zealand, but the elections in December 1949 denied both governments the opportunity to implement their policies on China. In Australia, Chifley was unseated and Liberal leader Robert Menzies returned to power.[25]

Curiously, the official historical record does not dwell on this glimmer of action in Australian China policy. The nine-hundred page Department of Foreign Affairs and Trade volume on the question of recognition from 1949–1972 does not reproduce any material from Chifley's time in office. It starts three months after the PRC was proclaimed, on 17 December 1949, with documents from the Menzies Government. There is no mention of the Australian reaction to the rise of Mao Zedong's Government, nor of the transfer the Australian Embassy initiated from Nanking to Peking. And Chifley's postponement of action until after the December election is excluded. These are striking omissions that recast the entire narrative of the volume.[26]

As Prime Minister, Menzies found himself with the same dilemma that Chifley had faced over China. He too toyed with the idea of recognition, but was hesitant to act while America and Britain adopted different policies towards China. The other big reason to refrain from immediate action was the personal crusade against domestic communism he had led during the election campaign. Although the two matters were separate, his Minister for External Affairs, Percy Spender, admitted the concern that 'they would be related in the minds of the people of Australia'.[27] As would happen so often over the course of the following two decades, domestic politics acted as a driving force of Australian international relations.

With the outbreak of the Korean War on 25 June 1950, Spender, uncertain of China's role in the conflict and the international reaction it would inspire, finally found a justification for the Government's hesitation on the question of recognition.[28]

The war in the 'near north' also gave new urgency to Australian negotiations for a regional security alliance. With the fall of Singapore in the Second World War, Australia had been made acutely aware that the British Empire, regardless of loyalty or kinship, could not necessarily come to Australia's aid in a time of crisis.[29] Australian policy makers needed another security alliance to give them confidence in what they saw as an unstable, unfriendly and unpredictable region. The United States was the obvious choice. With an alliance in mind, Spender took 'the utmost care' to align Australia's foreign policy with the United States whenever possible.[30] Whether the Americans directly told the Australian Government that non-recognition of the PRC was essential to a security pact is a matter of much speculation.[31] But with the establishment of the Australia, New Zealand, United States Security Treaty (ANZUS) in 1951 and the creation of the South East Asia Treaty Organisation (SEATO) in 1954, Australia's policy became increasingly tied to that of the United States. Recognition became a distant possibility.[32]

ANZUS fast became the main pillar of Australian defence and foreign policy, around which all other relationships grew. The treaty was a political coup for Australia, all the more so because it excluded Asian nations, to which Australia wanted no obligation. Australian policy makers did, however, want America to feel strong obligation towards the Asia-Pacific region and to commit to the defence of Australia. The same desire that drove the negotiations for ANZUS would later spur Australia to follow the US into the Vietnam War. This was not a decision of blind loyalty, but one based on Australia's own assessment of its interest: Australia wanted to see the West engaged in South East Asia at all costs.

The effects of ANZUS on Australian China policy were twofold. First, diplomatic ties with China were rendered impossible while America maintained its policy of hostility towards all communist nations. Second, a sense of loyalty towards nationalist China, rather than irritation or indifference, was now inherited from America. A 1958 review of Australian China policy by the Department for External Affairs established, in a striking declaration of servility, that Australia's 'diplomatic policy should not deviate from that of the United States.'[33] In the words of C.P. Fitzgerald, 'Australia found her policy towards China frozen at a time when it was still in formation.'[34]

II

Hostility

As the Cold War reached boiling point in the early 1950s, a new intensity bubbled over into Australian public debate about China. Traditional fears of a 'yellow peril' merged with the new international evil: the 'red menace'. Acknowledging the political existence of China's new *communist* government became out of the question, in spite of the fact that the PRC was home to a quarter of the world's population. We now turn to examine the language of hostility that filtered into Australia's political treatment of the PRC in the 1950s and 1960s.

'Politics', as anthropologist David I. Kertzer reminds us, 'is expressed through symbolism.'[35] These symbols have the power to enrich understanding, but also to distort reality and impart upon it a misplaced prism of assumptions and expectations. The most potent political symbols have a palpable quality to them; they transform concepts into real things and inspire real emotions. Take, for example, the enduring image of a 'rising tide of colour' spreading throughout Australia's empty north. This image has become grafted into Australian thinking about China; for more than a century it has not only dominated Australian fears but also shaped Australian policies.[36] The intensity and influence of such an image becomes strikingly clear through a brief glance at a time in Australian history when China was seen neither as an ominous unknown nor a looming threat.

'Until the 1840s', historian Eric Rolls writes, 'Australia had regarded trade and its subsequent social contract with China, India and South East Asia as a normal thing.'[37] China was viewed as a natural part of Australia's future. The imagery of a conniving and treacherous 'yellow peril' infiltrating and infecting Australia had yet to be conceived. Indeed, Sir Joseph Banks was one of many to suggest the Chinese as the perfect colonisers for the vast, empty land that had just been 'discovered'.[38] The seeds of prejudice against China were sowed on the Australian gold fields over anxieties about lowered wages and alongside changing ideas of race. The Chinese miners that arrived in waves in the 1850s and again in the 1870s were received with suspicion and were commonly depicted as the 'forerunners of a subtle invasion'. Their presence inspired resentment, inflamed anti-Chinese agitation and incited anti-Chinese legislation.[39] Australians were scared that the Chinese, by their sheer numbers, could overwhelm the country that European settlers had created. These colonial fears laid the rhetorical architecture for the anti-communist language that came to dominate the Australian Parliament in the 1950s and 1960s.

In 1954, Prime Minister Robert Menzies constructed the metaphoric template that would define Australia's Cold War experience. Menzies saw conspiracy in the very geography of Asia. Building on the oft-invoked image of communism crashing down from China, he described Australia as 'a democratic nation vitally at risk in these seas'. He characterised communist aggression as having the sole objective of expansion and achieving this through 'cunning or bloodshed, fraud and fury, with callous indifference to all moral and spiritual considerations'. He moved beyond traditional stereotypes and infused his speech with overtones of faith and morality, declaring the fight against communism to be 'a battle for the spirit of man'.[40] By elevating the conflict to spiritual dimensions he injected a new intensity into the traditional anti-Chinese discourse.

It was in this hostile climate of 1954 – indeed on the very same day as one parliamentarian labelled communism 'the worst evil that the world has ever known' and as coming 'from hell itself for the purpose of destroying the world' that Gough Whitlam first publicly endorsed political recognition of the PRC.[41]

When Whitlam entered the China conversation in August 1954, he was a young, ambitious man in only his second year of Parliament. Tall, silver-tongued, with thick dark hair slicked back over his scalp, Whitlam had already made a name for himself as a parliamentary performer. Some hailed him as prime ministerial material, an expectation that Gough Whitlam, with his seamless self-confidence, took in his stride.[42] But one thing that Whitlam could certainly not claim to be was a sinologist. Before entering politics he had little connection with China. His breadth of knowledge, however formidable, grew out of his very Western education in Law and Classics. Indeed, as James Curran has argued, it was this classical upbringing, and especially his deep appreciation of the Greco-Roman values of *logos*, *arete* and *humanitas*, that underpinned his regional outlook and internationalist vision.[43] It was not personal enthusiasm for Chinese culture that led him to advocate recognition of the PRC in 1954, but his passion for reason and his contempt of ideological distortions in international affairs.

In 2011, Stephen FitzGerald described to me Whitlam's conviction on the policy of recognition:

> He was convinced that it was right. That just in terms of the politics of it, it was right. He used to get quite indignant about the idea of us recognising Jiang Jieshi's Government in Taiwan as the sole government of China. With his mind, it was so illogical and politically unreal.[44]

For Whitlam, the continued support of an exiled minority government did not make sense, especially when it precluded recognising the political existence of the government of a quarter of the world's population. The irrationality of the policy riled him and he was determined to fix it.

On 12 August 1954, Whitlam not only attacked the Government's policies on China, but its whole approach to Australia's role in world affairs: 'The fact that for more than three years the House has not been allowed to participate in a debate on foreign affairs is a damning indictment of the Government.' His speech was a call for pragmatism, and he presented his case in a legalistic manner prefaced with statements such as 'Whether we like it or not' and 'We have to face the fact'. On that day, he became the first Member of Parliament to endorse diplomatic relations with the PRC and he did so 'in view of the fact that all our neighbours, including the colonial powers, Great Britain and the Netherlands, have recognized it.'[45]

Over the next eighteen years, Whitlam's campaign for political recognition was as consistent as it was constant.[46] His feelings were shared by many in his party, and they echoed the sentiments of the late Ben Chifley, who in 1951 had lamented the failure of his Government to recognise the PRC.[47] But the China issue was ultimately a divisive one for the Labor Party. Recognition lay at the heart of the traumatic factional split of 1954–55, which saw the expulsion of 'the small subversive clique' within Labor ranks – the Movement-Grouper forces – and the creation of the conservative Catholic and anti-communist Democratic Labor Party (DLP).[48] As the Archbishop of Melbourne and covert DLP supporter, Dr Daniel Mannix, put it, in the fierce rhetoric of the time:

> There are two Labor policies, that of Dr Evatt, who hastens to defend communists at home and abroad, and advocates recognition of Red China, and that of those who fight communism wherever possible as the enemy of God, Christianity and freedom.[49]

The ideological and sectarian differences could not be overcome. The Movement-Grouper forces broke away to form the DLP, while in March 1955, at a conflict-ridden conference in Hobart, recognition became ALP policy.[50] The formation of the DLP is important to this story, for the new party not only siphoned votes away from the ALP, further obstructing the path to government; it also played a significant role in the maintenance of a Cold War mentality in Australian politics. Throughout the 1950s and 60s the DLP's electoral preferences ensured that its views on foreign policy could not go unheeded by the Liberal/Country Party Government.[51] And in the DLP's eyes, recognition was out of the question; China was seen 'as the major threat to Australian interests – a foe who must be contained and restricted by every possible means.'[52]

Despite Whitlam's claims to 'realism', the metaphors and images constructed in Parliament about China and international communism should not be dismissed as mere rhetorical excesses; the intensity with which they were felt made them very real. It is only with this understanding that we can make sense of what former diplomat Alan Renouf describes as 'a baffling, irrational constancy' about Australia's foreign policy.[53] Throughout the 1950s and 60s Australian hostility towards China increased markedly, and with the Vietnam War it was vocalised with rhetoric that far exceeded that of the United States.[54] Unlike most officials in America, Australia attributed major responsibility to China for the conflict to their north. Vietnam was seen as a proxy war; China was the real enemy.[55] 'On such sublime idiocies', Gough Whitlam would declare in frustration, 'are great follies based.'[56]

An embassy in Taipei

In this chapter I have so far outlined prevailing patterns, but life unfolds in far from ordered ways and history is also about anomalies. Prime Minister Harold Holt's decision to establish an embassy in nationalist China on 11 June 1966 is exemplary of this fact. Whitlam characterised it as 'one of the oddest episodes in our history' and it does indeed stand out in Australian China policy, if only as a rare, decisive action against a background of dithering.[57] Australia-Taiwan specialist Gary Klintworth claims that it was a strategic decision driven by pressures from the Australia-America alliance and a continuing fear of communist China. But the posting made little strategic sense, especially considering the new language of 'reconciliation' the US President Lyndon Johnson was to announce in July 1966.[58] It was a decision made against the advice of the Minister for External Affairs, Paul Hasluck, and it caused general dismay within his Department.[59] While it is true that the history of this embassy should not be dismissed as a mere outlier – an unimportant footnote in Australian relations with Asia – it is also unhelpful to search for a trend that justifies Holt's decision 'as the result of a longer-term shift'.[60] The embassy seemed to be effected more on the basis of a personal friendship between Holt and the Taiwanese Ambassador in Canberra, Chen Zhimai, than anything else.[61]

Later in the year, an Australian delegation in London expressed to their hosts their despair at Holt's actions, declaring that 'Australia had gone and burned her own boats by linking herself closely with the Jiang Jieshi regime, which had no political future.'[62] The imprudent nature of this decision was compounded by what the Australian delegation described as the 'changing attitude towards the Chinese People's Republic' at the United Nations and 'in American official thinking'.[63]

The full significance of these comments needs to be unpacked. They demonstrate a strong awareness within the Department of External Affairs in 1966 of a shift in America's policy towards China. That is to say, one full year before a US Presidential hopeful by the name of Richard Nixon broadcast the 'new chapter' he envisaged for American engagement with Asia in his now landmark essay 'Asia after Viet Nam'.[64] And three years before Nixon, as President, announced America's retreat from Asia and started overt initiatives to normalise relations with the PRC.[65] Regardless of how much Australia claimed to align its China policy with that of America, the establishment of an embassy in Taiwan and the continued hostility towards communist China into the early 1970s were independent courses of action. As Roderic Pitty has argued with attention to the American initiatives in 1969, Australia was caught 'way behind in following the USA over China'.[66]

III

The wheat stoppage

As early as 1950, deputy Labor leader H.V. Evatt had publicly argued that Australian recognition of the PRC would be 'an enormous advantage from the trading point of view'.[67] In 1959 the Country Party made a very similar case, though pressure from the DLP forced them to drop the policy.[68] But even without the establishment of diplomatic relations, business boomed between the two countries. While America put an embargo on all trade with mainland China from 1949 to 1969, Australia developed a lucrative trade in wool and wheat with its northern neighbour.[69] The contrasting images of 'China the traditional enemy' and 'China the good customer' were balanced with the assertion that Australia did not mix trade and politics.[70]

Ironically, some of the most energetic advocates for relations with the PRC were also the most vocal in their anti-Chinese sentiment. John McEwen, leader of the Australian Country Party, typified this paradox. Despite his deeply-felt anti-communist views, McEwen was instrumental in taking Australia's trading relationship with communist China to another level. As Minister for Trade, McEwen oversaw a dramatic rise in Australian wheat exports, with a million metric tons being sold to China between December 1960 and January 1961. By 1962–63, China bought more than half of Australia's wheat exports, and by the end of the decade China was buying a third of Australia's total wheat production.[71] There was, of course, a sinister (and suppressed) story behind China's demand for wheat. Mao Zedong, with his disastrous Great Leap Forward, had imposed upon the people of China the largest famine in human history.

The wheat contract signed in December 1969 was for 2.2 million metric tons of wheat – the largest order yet. But instead of trade continuing to expand between the two nations, in October 1970 it abruptly stopped. The season had brought China record harvests and even a small grain reserve. After years of agrarian crisis, Chinese officials now had the luxury of choice among their trading partners.[72] Some attribute China's decision to stop importing Australian wheat to inflammatory comments made by the Minister for External Affairs, Gordon Freeth. On 14 June 1969, Freeth spoke from Hong Kong of 'serious questionings of conscience in Australia about how far we're justified in trading with China'.[73] Although the insult invited the scorn of Chinese Trade Officials, it cannot be isolated as the cause of the wheat stoppage: the cessation of trade was a symptom of deeper policy differences and of a rapidly changing international scene.

October 1970 – the date of the anticipated renewal of Australia's wheat contract – is significant for another reason. It was in this month that Canada, after two years of negotiations and a long personal crusade by liberal Prime Minister Pierre Elliott Trudeau, finally agreed upon the terms under which it would extend political recognition to the PRC.[74] Under the 'One China' formula, Canada would recognise the communist government in Peking as 'the sole Government of China', as opposed to Australia's 'Two China' policy, which also recognised Jiang Jieshi's regime in Taiwan. While the Australian Wheat Board unsuccessfully sought to negotiate a new contract with China, Canada secured its largest trade deal yet.[75] China did mix trade and politics.

The new diplomatic relations established between Canada and the PRC were but one sign of a more active and outward looking foreign policy pursued by China. The most violent and turbulent period of the Cultural Revolution had subsided and across the country a gradual social and economic reconstruction was taking place.[76] Since 1969, China had increased its international presence in terms of trade, re-despatched ambassadors abroad, and opened its borders to visiting national delegations.[77] In the words of William McMahon, the new Minister of the renamed Department of Foreign Affairs, China was presenting a 'smiling face' to the international community in an attempt 'to reassert herself as a world power'.[78] Importantly for Whitlam, Canada's actions gave him a formula with which he could apply the ALP's long-held policy of recognition.

China surged back into public debate in Australia. The burst of international activity and the controversy surrounding the wheat stoppage were joined by a domestic groundswell.[79] Recognition of the PRC was becoming increasingly popular, fuelled by the growing anti-Vietnam War movement and a moral myth that surrounded Mao, casting communist China in a utopian light. A Gallup Poll held on 6 October 1970 showed that 49 percent of Australians were now in favour of recognition and only 35 percent opposed.[80] In light of all these developments, and with particular attention to Nixon's changing perspectives towards Peking, in November 1970 McMahon ordered the first review of Australia's China policy since 1958.[81]

The document presents a fascinating insight into what McMahon, the primary author of the review, and his Department, were thinking about Australian China policy in the months before he became Prime Minister.[82] He recognised the new surge of international support for the PRC and did not want to be left in its wake. 'The guiding consideration in our approach to this issue', he wrote in February 1971, 'should be the prejudice we will suffer should we stand still rather than any advantages we might gain if we move.'[83] He showed an awareness of the overtures that Nixon was making towards China as well as of the prophetic belief amongst high-level Chinese officials that any improvement between the two nations would come about 'all at once'. Such a breakthrough he deemed 'unlikely in the near future, but not impossible.'

The review was a call to action on China policy. It acknowledged that if the Government continues its 'present policy we will court disadvantages in trade as well as politically.' It recommended movement on the China question, but fell short of endorsing a policy of recognition. McMahon's reasons for hesitation were threefold. Not only would it look bad domestically (considering the Labor Party's policy), but it also might weaken the United States' bargaining position with China. Furthermore, there would be no guarantee the establishment of diplomatic relations would benefit trade; it was deemed quite likely that the PRC was aiming for self-sufficiency. 'We cannot, in short, go too far too quickly along the road to recognition', McMahon concluded.

What is perhaps most striking about this document is that, although it is a review of China policy, the primary focus rests on the movements of the Americans and the Japanese and international trends, not China. Indeed, when China is discussed it is in similar language to the Cold War rhetoric of Menzies and the DLP; it is portrayed as a wild, malevolent beast that needs to be 'tamed' and which 'can be expected to discriminate against us (Australia) whenever possible on political grounds.'[84] The continuing currency of these stereotypes reveals how little first-hand knowledge there was about China in the Department of Foreign Affairs.[85] Their continuation also explains how Australian politicians, such as the new Minister for Trade and Industry, Doug Anthony, could speak with such brazen hostility about the Chinese. Anthony's declaration in March 1971 that 'I would not sell my soul just to benefit trade' joined Freeth's comments of two years earlier and further damaged

Australia's reputation in China.[86] Now, more than ever, the Chinese did not want to conduct a trade in wheat with Australia. As so often was the case, in Alison Broinowski's words, 'politics in Australia sided with history and against geography, even to the detriment of economics.'[87]

The genesis of a visit: 'Ping-pong diplomacy'

In the weeks that followed McMahon's review, China again showed its 'smiling face', offering a famous token of friendship to the international community. Invitations were sent out across the world, including to America and Australia, to participate in the thirty-first World Table Tennis Championships held over April-May in Peking.[88] The gesture caused a media storm and was heralded as 'ping-pong diplomacy'. It came to symbolise a new era of political possibility in international affairs.

Amidst these developments, the Australian Liberal Party, divided and in disarray, underwent its third leadership change in six years.[89] John Gorton made way for the dapper party elder William McMahon. McMahon was sixty-three when he came to power and he brought to office more ministerial experience than anyone before or since. This, however, was not a fact in his favour. Many thought of him as 'more ministerial than prime ministerial' and, as his biographer Julian Leeser is at pain to stress, 'his term as prime minister was probably the least rewarding of his career.'[90] Short, bald, with large ears and a 'tremulous, piping voice', McMahon liked to be known as 'Bill', but was more often referred to as 'Billy'. I use his full name, 'William', in this book, and I do it in some small way to challenge the caricature that he has become. As Peter Sekuless points out, McMahon is somewhat to blame for his poor posthumous reputation.[91] He never published his memoirs and he has frustrated historians by closing access to his personal papers, thus denying himself a full-length biography where his weaknesses could be weighed against his strengths. Instead, he is remembered for his political gaffs, his vivacious younger wife, and a suite of unkind cartoons penned by the likes of Bruce Petty and Larry Pickering.

As a minister, McMahon had proven himself to be a capable and hard working administrator, but as a leader he struggled to hold the party together at a time of adversity. He lacked Whitlam's flair, had difficulty delegating responsibilities and was uncannily accident-prone.[92] One of his ministers, Peter Howson, writing in January 1972, despaired at McMahon's 'foibles and weakness of character':

> Bill McMahon is not an easy Prime Minister with whom to work. How often one would like to be firm and tell him what one thinks, but then one has to remember that we put him there, that he's got to be supported.[93]

McMahon came to power at the Liberal Party's least promising moment. The 1969 election had seen an enormous 6.5 per cent swing against Gorton, an emphatic sign of the electorate's desire for political change. The party was dispirited and after the demise of Gorton as leader it had 'an air of disorganisation at times verging on panic'.[94] For the Australian Labor Party, the moment was ripe for political exploitation.

The Federal Secretary of the ALP, Mick Young, came up with the plan that he hoped would both embarrass the new Prime Minister over the wheat stoppage and advance Labor's long-held policy of recognition.[95] His daring proposal was met by the Labor Executive with unanimous support and Opposition Leader Gough Whitlam followed it up immediately, sending an historic telegram to the Chinese Premier Zhou Enlai:

> Australian Labor Party anxious to send delegation to People's Republic of China to discuss the terms on which

your government is interested in having diplomatic and trade relations with Australia.[96]

The telegram was the first political contact with Peking since 1954, when R.G. Casey, as Minister for External Affairs, had met briefly with the Chinese Premier in Geneva.[97] If the response was positive, Whitlam would become the first Western leader to visit the People's Republic of China since its inauguration in 1949.

The initiative was announced the following day, on 15 April. Gough Whitlam located the telegram within the broader pattern of his own Asia-oriented foreign policy, which prioritised regionalism and internationalism over ties with 'great and powerful friends'. He seized the opportunity to lambast the Government's actions on China as 'supine' and, in a rare statement from an Australian politician, he accorded similar criticism to the United States. 'Friendly nations like Canada and Italy', he stated, 'have helped America off the hook.' He hoped that his initiative, like the acts of ping-pong diplomacy, would cast off the fear and ideology which clouded Australian China policy and be a step 'towards diplomatic sanity in the Pacific'.[98]

In the press, Whitlam's telegram to Zhou was portrayed as a political reaction to the wheat stoppage; to many Labor members this was all it had ever been. For McMahon, it was an unexpected challenge. He responded by denouncing the visit and using the opportunity to reiterate Government support for nationalist China.[99] Why, we must wonder, did he strongly support the legitimacy of the exiled nationalist regime when so recently, as Foreign Minister, he had stressed the 'unreality' and 'insubstantial pretension' of Jiang Jieshi's position? Despite his recent recommendation for a change in Australia's policy towards China, McMahon chose to toe the party line for two reasons. First, he needed to unite the party under his leadership. As historian Edmund S.K. Fung argues, 'McMahon naturally understood that it would be political disaster for him to depart radically from old premises, even if he wanted to, unless he had the Liberal Party fully behind him.'[100] Second, he could not afford to lose the electoral preferences of the Democratic Labor Party, whose members were fiercely against recognition and which, at the start of the 1970s, was at the peak of its power.[101] The other reason – and this will be more fully explored in chapter three – was psychological. It was difficult for many Australians to come to terms with a region which for so long had been perceived as their nemesis.

Talking with two voices

One of Whitlam's private secretaries, Richard Hall, set to work stressing the seriousness of the request to China through every non-communist channel available to him.[102] One of the 'friends of China' that Hall contacted was Australian expat and Harvard sinologist Ross Terrill, who was invigorated by the idea of a Labor party visit to Peking. Terrill followed up on the cable through contacts in Hong Kong and Canada, before finally getting a breakthrough with his connection to the well-known and well-liked French Ambassador in Peking, Etienne Manac'h.[103] After acquainting him with Australia's domestic situation, Terrill asked Manac'h if he would have 'an informal word at some stage' and convey to the Chinese the political importance and diplomatic possibilities of the Australian invitation.[104] The contact through Manac'h proved invaluable.

On 8 May Manac'h was able to approach a senior official, Han Xu, on a personal plane, who then relayed the substance of Terrill's message to Zhou Enlai.[105] Such is the convoluted nature of non-diplomatic channels. Two days after Manac'h's intervention, a telegram arrived for Gough Whitlam. It was from the People's Institute of Foreign Affairs, a body used by the PRC for contacts with non-recognising nations, and it invited an ALP delegation to China.[106] The distant possibility of travelling to China suddenly reared into reality. For Whitlam, the political risks were intense. Unsure of whether he should send his Shadow Minister for Agriculture, Dr Rex Patterson, or lead the party himself, Whitlam called his close friend and press secretary, Graham Freudenberg, for advice. 'Do you think I should go?' he asked. Freudenberg weighed up the advantages and disadvantages and concluded that it was too big a risk. But by the time the two men met later that day, both had changed their minds and Whitlam approached his friend with the words: 'I want you to come too.'[107]

The whole process took almost four weeks, which, Stephen FitzGerald notes, 'by comparison with the response to similar requests from other countries was quite prompt.'[108] In retrospect the delay worked to Labor's advantage. Not only had it allowed the public to get used to the idea, but it earned Whitlam even more political initiative. The McMahon Government had capitalised on the four weeks of uncertainty to ridicule Whitlam's telegram. But now that the delegation was going ahead, he was forced to change his strategy on China. On receiving news of the invitation, on May 11, McMahon made a statement in front of the press. Putting aside his rich collection of veiled titles for China – 'continental China', 'mainland China', 'Peking China', 'communist China' – he declared that he was now willing to 'explore the possibilities of establishing a dialogue with the People's Republic (of China).'[109] By the end of the month he had opened a conversation with the Chinese through representatives in Paris. His goal: to 'work towards the normalisation of relations through the establishment of commercial, cultural and other ties.'[110] Although the initiative appears superficial and reactionary, some credit should be given to McMahon. Unlike Whitlam, who was boldly capitalising on a policy he had expounded for seventeen years, McMahon's small step towards China was a traumatic change to established Liberal policy. After twenty-two years of apathy, ambivalence and hostility, Australia was talking to communist China. Only now it had two voices.

A train ride from Hong Kong

It is Friday 2 July 1971. After five long hot days in Hong Kong, the ALP delegation is on the verge of entering China. The visit is already being heavily mythologised by Whitlam, who has audaciously proclaimed to the accompanying press that it 'is easily the most significant mission undertaken by a political party from a Western country.'[111] Certainly, it is not only an important Australian moment – Whitlam is the first Western leader to travel to the PRC since its inauguration in 1949, a fact that will not elude his Chinese hosts.[112] More tellingly, though, the hyperbole of the statement illustrates the hope that surrounds the visit. The delegation's high spirits will not even be dampened by the announcement of the Chinese Minister for Foreign Trade that 'China would continue to consider Canada first as a source of wheat as import needs arose.'[113] In Whitlam's eyes, the visit has assumed a far greater purpose than solving the wheat stoppage. It is now a test to see if the people of China and the people of Australia are able to talk to and understand each other after more than twenty years of separation.[114] 'Australia will learn more about China in the next 14 days than ever previously', Whitlam stridently declares to the accompanying press.[115]

As the sun blazes above, the Australians huddle on a local train to the border village of Lo Wu. It is loaded with housewives and workers, vendors selling cigarettes and youths looking to escape the heat with a swim.[116] A vast landscape, rich with greens and gold, streams past the window. Peasants wearing broad hats and carrying bundles work the fields while boys run and call out to the passing carriages. After weeks of messy internal 'power politics' over who should travel with Whitlam to China, six men find themselves on the train as part of the official delegation. Alongside Young, Patterson, Whitlam and Freudenberg, sits Tom Burns, the Federal President of the ALP, and Stephen FitzGerald, a China expert from the ANU working as the delegation's 'advisor, interpreter and smoother-of-the-way'.[117] Terrill, who helped obtain the invitation, is waiting to meet them in Peking.

Accompanying the delegation are nine journalists.[118] It had been a long fight to secure them all visas. When the documentation finally came through, the Australians collected the visas from the China Travel Service in Kowloon. An eight-foot long banner flanked the door of the building, exhorting 'Peoples of the world unite to defeat the US aggressors and their running dogs.'[119] Was Australia one of these hated 'running dogs'? This is a question that does not escape the group of Australians who feel nervous as well as excited about the coming days.[120]

The train begins to slow and then comes to a halt. The Australians disembark at Lo Wu, clear British immigration procedures, and then step onto a narrow wooden footbridge which straddles the border between Hong Kong and China. The time is 11.55 am. Some of the men are wearing open necked shirts; Whitlam carries the jacket of his suit over his arm.[121] The crossing is something of a novelty for the local press who eagerly snap photos of the delegation. Some of these journalists speculate in their newspapers that this is the last the world will hear of the delegation.[122] The uncertain fate of the journalist Francis James must have loomed in the Australians' minds. James, Whitlam's old schoolmate, disappeared at this very border twenty months earlier, on 4 November 1969.

When Ross Terrill walked the footbridge two weeks earlier, he was in a philosophical mood. He mused, in words that echoed the diaries of Frederic Eggleston, that

> There really *are* 'two Chinas'. Not 'Taiwan' and the 'Mainland', but rather the *image* we have of China ... and the *reality* of China. Our press talks of China as power struggles and bombs and numbers. But here is China as rice and heat, glue and vaccinations, babies crying, old men playing chess ... The cardboard figures of a frozen scenario start to breathe and sweat and make noise.[123]

As the Australians cross into the township of Shumchun, the 'shimmering mirage' of China – the China constructed in their minds – grows indistinct. Behind them lies a land of certainty and control, familiar commercialism and lines of communication with the outside world. Before them is the unknown.

Top: **Whitlam talks with Zhou Enlai in the Great Hall of the People, 5 July 1971**
National Archives of Australia: M155, B22

Bottom: **Henry Kissinger shakes Zhou Enlai's hand, 9 July 1971**
Associated Press

Chapter Two

Barbarians in the Middle Kingdom

A Tale of Two Visits, July 1971

'For generations the Chinese regarded themselves as the flowers of the Flowery Land while those across the wide sea were the barbarians.'

Eric Rolls, *Sojourners: The epic story of China's centuries-old relationship with Australia.*[1]

After Canada extended political recognition to the People's Republic of China under the 'One China' formula in October 1970, a parade of nations followed suit. In China, the acts of 'ping-pong diplomacy' were immediately followed by the Canton International Trade Fair, and by the time of the Australian delegation's arrival the Chinese had been almost constant hosts, meeting with leaders and representatives from Peru, Malaysia, the Philippines, Romania, Yugoslavia, Italy, Nepal, Pakistan, Somalia, Sudan, Congo, Cuba, Chad and Mongolia – to name a few. As the Chinese borders bustled with incoming traffic, the Foreign Ministry also dispatched forty-five Ambassadors abroad and engaged in lengthy discussions in Mali, Guinea and even, despite their bitter recent history, the

Soviet Union. The sudden burst of activity was a statement to the international community. China's new outward-looking diplomatic style was attracting attention. It seemed increasingly likely that, in the impending vote of October 1971, the PRC would finally be admitted to the United Nations General Assembly.[2] The list of nations recognising the PRC was also lengthening. Representatives from Britain, Japan, New Zealand, Turkey, Tunisia and Burundi had signalled their intentions to visit China in the near future.[3] A delegation from the Australian Labor Party had just left for Peking. Even the American President, Richard Nixon, had apparently offhandedly mentioned his desire to visit China.[4] The barbarians from across the wide sea were storming the Middle Kingdom, and the Chinese were holding the door wide open.

Considering this surge of international activity around China, and the language of 'inevitability' that Gough Whitlam so often harnessed, it would be easy for us to retrospectively strip such individual visits of their significance. Indeed, some, such as Joseph Camilleri, are guilty of this when they dismiss the whole of Whitlam's foreign policy as an 'adaptive reaction' to international trends more than a conscious and coherent attempt at revision.[5] The influence of the international context is important, but so too are the motives of individual visits. Whitlam's visit to China came at the end of a long and consistent campaign for recognition. When put in the international context it appears more judicious than radical, but in the Australian context, and especially in relation to the faltering conservatism of the McMahon Government, it was a bold step. And as for 'inevitability', Whitlam is right when, on the first page of his political memoirs, he asserts: 'in politics nothing is inevitable, least of all change.'[6] This chapter will look at two agents of change and their daring visits to China in July 1971.

The events of this month are familiar to many, mostly as part of a clipped narrative, high on drama, and low on description. This chapter explores the texture of these two visits. It anchors the political drama in human events. What did happen in China between 2 and 14 July that lifted this moment out of the halls of history and into the leaves of legend? The narrative unfolds in three parts. First, it explores the impressions of the visitors and the reactions of their hosts. Second, it unpacks the centre-piece of the visit: a high-stakes political conversation in the Great Hall of the People. Finally, it probes the act of secret diplomacy that irrevocably transformed the page upon which this story is written.

I

'A hug and an apology in Peking'

The heavy heat of a Peking summer lingered well into the evening on Wednesday 7 July 1971. A crowd of more than one hundred thousand sweated close together in the Peking Workers' Stadium as they watched the Albanian soccer team clash with China. In the VIP box, the Albanian Ambassador sat tensely beside the Chinese Premier, Zhou Enlai. They were joined by a variety of other officials, including the visiting delegation from the Australian Labor Party.

The match was a curious spectacle. As one Australian journalist, Kenneth Randall, commented, it 'was marked by a degree of politeness and goodwill unbelievable to Australian sporting crowds.'[7] The players hugged one another before and after the match, and each infringement of the rules was accompanied by a handshake. The pace of the game was slow and the play appeared restricted, especially the tackling. The peculiar politeness even extended to the crowd; the Chinese spectators did not openly support either team, but commended a good movement by either side with restrained applause.

Fittingly, the match ended in a 1-1 draw, with no injuries to either side. We should by no means assume that this was a coincidence. As American table tennis player Connie Sweeris had experienced earlier in the year with the matches of 'ping-pong diplomacy', the emphasis had been heavily on 'diplomacy', not sport: 'even though the Chinese players were the best in the world, they let us win a few games. Table tennis bridged the gap between us.'[8] When President Nixon did eventually visit China, although he had never played table tennis before, he scored fourteen points before losing to his opponent, Chairman Mao Zedong.

It is in sport that the theatre of diplomacy is laid bare; the delicate game of tact loses some of its subtlety and the elaborate rituals of negotiation are exposed. Since his arrival days earlier, Whitlam had found himself walking a tightrope in his discussions with the Chinese. 'There was warmth', he wrote with Freudenberg in *The Australian*,

> but there was wariness. And not surprisingly. A generation of
> mutual incomprehension is not to be dissipated overnight or
> in a visit of two weeks for that matter.[9]

Although he had no contact with the outside world, Whitlam knew that the eyes of the Australian press would be upon him and he was anxious to assert himself in Peking. He needed this visit to be a success. And he was aware that he would not only have to perform for the press; in myriad ways, the Chinese were quietly testing him and his delegation.

The Australians had flown into Peking near midnight on 3 July after an exhausting five-hour flight from Canton through 'a prolonged and spectacular thunderstorm'.[10] They were met at the airport by representatives from the People's Institute for Foreign Affairs and shuttled to their luxurious hotel, a kilometre east of the Great Hall of the People.[11] Peking Hotel, with its handsome wooden floors and vast, ornate windowsills, was normally reserved for official guests only. Despite representing a political party, not a nation, the delegation would evidently be accorded full VIP treatment. In the foyer of the hotel, beside a giant white statue of Chairman Mao Zedong, their host, Chou Chui-yeh, noted the Australians' weariness and suggested the men take the next day, a Sunday, to rest and visit the Great Wall. Whitlam immediately cut him off with the purposeful statement: 'No. We have come here to work.'[12] It set the mood for the visit.

The following day, at 9 am, Whitlam plunged into an intensive two-and-a-half hour discussion with Acting Foreign Minister Ji Pengfei. Whitlam led the talks with energy and determination, presenting ALP policy and seeking assurance from Ji that Peking and Canberra would be able to establish diplomatic relations on the 'Canada Formula'. (That is, recognising Taiwan as a province of the PRC as opposed to a separate state or, as was the policy of the McMahon Government, the sole government of China.) There was, of course, a big difference between Australia and Canada: Australia had an embassy in Taipei, Canada did not. If you gain office, Ji asked Whitlam, what will you do about that? 'I will not send an Ambassador to Taipei', Whitlam replied.[13] When pressed, he promised to 'withdraw' the embassy from Taipei. Whitlam's evident non-regard for Jiang Jieshi's regime appealed to Ji, but this did not lead to any immediate concessions on the part of the Chinese.

The following morning the Chinese Trade Minister, Bai Xiangguo, stressed to the Australians the importance of 'One China' recognition before the wheat trade could be continued between the two countries. Dr Rex Patterson led the meeting on this occasion and although he was frustrated not to have made progress on the question of the wheat stoppage, he did confirm with Bai that Australia's major trade prospects following diplomatic recognition rested with iron, steel, bauxite and, much to the Queenslander's excitement, sugar.

Both meetings had all the appearance of formality. On Sunday the men sat in a room with lush red carpet in the Foreign Ministry reception building; on Monday talks were held in the grand hall at Number 42 Anti-Imperialist Road. Yet, as one journalist put it, there was 'an ephemeral, conditional quality about the whole exercise.'[14] Both Ji and Bai were careful in their talks not to burn China's bridges with the McMahon Government. They demonstrated a strong understanding of Australian domestic politics and were aware that McMahon had just asked the Australian Ambassador in Paris, Alan Renouf, to continue exploratory talks with his Chinese counterpart, Huang Chen.[15]

The dialogue in Paris, however, had reached an impasse. Renouf had been ordered to discuss trade and cultural ties – anything but the question of diplomatic recognition; Huang's instructions were precisely the reverse.[16] On Saturday 3 July McMahon announced the progress of the Paris talks to a televised press conference in Perth. 'We have not been able to get any common sense out of [the Chinese]', he declared, drawing on the rich pool of stereotypes about the 'inscrutability' of the Chinese: 'They move slowly and according to their own interests. Very seldom do they move in accordance with the wishes of those who might wish to establish sensible relations.'[17] Official recognition, he concluded, was still a fair way off.

Whitlam, on the other hand, was happy with his first two days of meetings. The news on recognition and the wheat trade were as he had expected. (As he would later explain, 'the blunt fact is that Australia has no exceptional leverage in Peking. We have nothing to offer which China desperately or especially wants.'[18]) And his talks with Chinese ministers had given him the opportunity to settle a few issues on his mind. For example, he had been anxious to know what would happen about China's current ties with the Australian Maoists if the two countries were to exchange ambassadors. 'Non-interference' was the policy, Ji replied: 'We do not know what is best for Australia.'[19] On the question of US-China relations, Ji was frank with Whitlam: 'Taiwan is the crux.'[20] Whitlam had even gained the concession that Australia, under his leadership, could continue to trade with Taiwan through *non-governmental* agencies.

The ALP delegation had obviously impressed the Chinese. They had been granted serious discussions with Ministers of importance.[21] But Whitlam was still unsure whether he would gain an audience with the Chinese Premier, Zhou Enlai. He was disappointed that such a meeting had not been included in the itinerary prepared by the People's Institute of Foreign Affairs. But he remained ever hopeful.[22]

Sojourners

As a group, the Australians somewhat bewildered their Chinese hosts. The journalists and the official delegation knew each other well from the Press Gallery and, for the most part, they mixed together and travelled as one.[23] Walsh, Young and Burns kept up the spirits of the delegation with lively chatter and enjoyed confusing their Chinese interpreters with a very distinctive brand of rhyming slang. In his political memoirs, Whitlam offers us an example: 'We had to spend long periods waiting at airports for the weather to clear for our Ilyushin 18s to take off or land. This became "waiting for the optical".'[24] Everyone and everything got nicknames. One of the interpreters who accompanied the delegation throughout their trip, Wei Jianye, was cheekily referred to as 'Milky'. ('Wei' is pronounced 'Way'.) The Australian sense of humour did not help understanding of the already troublesome Australian accent, which was 'a thing of terror' to Chinese ears familiar with English spoken by Americans.[25] Perhaps it is no surprise that, in the words of Freudenberg, the Australians 'appeared stranger creatures to the Chinese than what they appeared to us.'[26]

Yet, although they were outsiders, and despite being escorted everywhere they went, the experience of the delegation in China was far from superficial. As Stephen FitzGerald reflected in 1976, on return from his posting as Australia's first Ambassador to the PRC,

> It is possible to find out more about China as a diplomat than
> it is to find out about other countries as a diplomat. This is
> precisely because the visitor – or the sojourner in China – is
> expected to inform himself of the country, the society and the
> way in which it functions.[27]

Their Chinese hosts showed off their country at every opportunity
and Whitlam, like Frederic Eggleston before him, embraced the
tradition of the sojourner. 'His mind is like a beam whose ray
must cast itself somewhere', Ross Terrill wrote in 1971, 'Between
talks with Chinese leaders, he plunged into social or historical
investigation, now with a question and now with an answer to
someone else's question, but at all times engaged with China as
if no other country existed on earth.'[28] He devoured the books on
Chinese culture that FitzGerald supplied him with and approached
all aspects of his travelling experience with great enthusiasm,
whether he was explaining the details of Chinese dynasties to the
accompanying journalists or downing the explosive rice wine, *mao-
t'ai*. His 'boundless energy' and insatiable intellectual curiosity
fuelled and encouraged the whole party.[29]

The journalists shared his sense of adventure about the whole
enterprise and their presence proved crucial to the success of the
visit. (Although, as Terrill observed, 'it puzzled [the Chinese] that
Australian papers sent political correspondents, not foreign policy
or Asian specialists.'[30]) Importantly, the stories that filtered back
to Australia gave the public rare insights into a forbidden and
unknown land. Very few Australians had travelled to China. And
although the delegation had a political edge, its members were
aware of the rare opportunity afforded to them and were intent on
learning as much as possible about the land and its culture.[31]

The Australians did eventually reach the Great Wall and, in the
heat of the day, marched its mighty contours dressed in white.[32]
On the return they passed the Ming tombs and over the course
of the following days they toured the Forbidden City, witnessed

the intricacies of Chinese acupuncture and, as a special mark of esteem by their hosts, were granted a rare tour of a new oil refinery outside Peking. (The Romanian delegation headed by President Nicolae Ceauşescu had been allowed the only other inspection of the refinery.)[33] In the evenings they were treated with film screenings, expeditions to the ballet and opera, and lavish banquets with Chinese and Western dignitaries.[34]

The hospitality of their escorts from the People's Institute of Foreign Affairs knew no bounds. They were attentive to the wants and needs of the Australians and catered to these where possible. The Australian enthusiasm for Chinese beer, for example, did not escape the eyes of their hosts, who soon began to serve it at every occasion, including breakfast.[35] But the Chinese hospitality extended beyond dietary needs and physical comforts. As FitzGerald later wrote, 'the Chinese went out of their way to provide everything that was essential to the success of the visit, in the A.L.P'.s terms as much as their own.'[36] This was never more evident than on the evening of Monday 5 July.

II

'Centre-stage with the maestro'

After a morning of talks with Bai Xiangguo, and just before lunch, the Australians were asked by the spokesman for the People's Institute to 'please remain in the hotel': there would be an 'interesting film' that evening. He did not explain why, but they would need to be formally dressed for the occasion. The hours passed and no further information came until late in the afternoon, when the official returned. The film was off. 'Sometime in the night', he announced, barely able to suppress his excitement, 'you will be taken to see the Premier.'[37]

It was a coup for the Australians and they immediately peppered the official with questions. The meeting, he divulged, would be held privately in the Great Hall of the People, and probably not until quite late. Zhou Enlai, at the age of seventy-three, had a formidable reputation, both as a worker and an intellect. A night owl, he worked most days until four or five in the morning. Midnight meetings were common practice.

The summons came earlier than expected. At 9 pm the Australian journalists left the hotel, and soon after the official delegation followed.[38] They were driven to the front steps of the monolithic, stone structure of the Great Hall of the People, which even today emanates a powerful sense of grandeur. It looms tall above the vast, empty expanse of Tiananmen Square and is flanked on one side by the impressive doors of the Forbidden City. Whitlam was led past the Red Army guards and through the high ceiling lobbies to the sparsely furnished East Room.[39] There, he found the small, slim figure of Zhou Enlai.

The Premier greeted the Australians individually in English. Then, after the customary photographs with the delegation, he surprised the travelling pressmen by inviting them to stay and 'bear witness to the fact that the people of China want to be friends with the people of Australia.'[40] His words transformed the supposedly 'private' meeting into a public performance, staged in front of Australian and Chinese press and a dozen television cameras. It was an act of tactical finesse and a fundamental component of what Stephen FitzGerald has tentatively termed 'guerrilla diplomacy'.[41] This is not to suggest that Whitlam was ambushed by the Chinese, or that they approached the discussions in a hostile fashion; it is rather to highlight the strategy of the event. On the surface a diplomatic meeting may appear to be all 'hugs' and 'goodwill', as was the nature of the contest between Albania and China at the Peking Workers' Stadium; but at a deeper level, an intricate battle of wits is being fought. By asking the press to stay, Zhou was issuing a challenge to the Australian Opposition Leader.

Whitlam's initial unease was palpable. Every word he said that evening would be read and analysed in Australia and around the world. 'The political risks became intense', Whitlam later wrote, recalling his nerves.[42] The twenty Australian and Chinese journalists joined forty officials who were already in the room, sitting expectantly in a horseshoe of cane chairs.[43] Whitlam took his seat next to Zhou Enlai at the centre of this scene. Beside him sat the official members of the ALP delegation; beside Zhou sat many of the Ministers and senior aides the Australians had met in the past two days.

I will devote some time to dissecting this meeting. The 105 minutes spent in that grand room with crimson carpets and opulent chandeliers defined the political outcome of the visit. It is the centrepiece of this drama. And this is precisely because the Chinese chose to make it so. Why, we must wonder, did the Chinese grant such a high-level meeting to a visiting delegation from the Australian Opposition? The timing is one reason. The publicity of the event and the obscurity of his rival gave Zhou Enlai the opportunity to broadcast internationally his views of the contemporary world situation. In the unfolding discussion, Sino-Australian relations took a secondary position on the agenda: Zhou meant for his statements to be heard in Tokyo, Moscow and, especially, Washington. Another reason is the importance China now attached to relations with 'small powers', like Australia. The new outward-looking foreign policy that China had been cultivating in 1970–71 was focused largely on building ties with 'small powers', including those of the 'second world'.[44] It was only through increased international participation of 'small powers', Zhou reasoned, that the dominating and dangerous bipolar environment that had been created by America and Russia could be defused. Their involvement would also be needed to avoid Nixon's envisaged five-power configuration of world politics – between the US, China, Western Europe, the Soviet Union and Japan – which Zhou believed to be hegemonic and opposed to his cherished principle of sovereign equality.[45]

Leaning back in his wicker chair, Zhou sat relaxed and at ease in this public environment. His arms rested limply beside him, becoming animated at intervals for effect: there was little wasted motion, either in his words or his actions.[46] Whitlam, at a comparatively gargantuan six feet four, sat stiffly beside him, leaning forward in the chair, his hands clasped: a giant hunched in concentration. The exchange was polite, but blunt. Whitlam's direct style suited the Premier's own. Having led most of his discussions with the Chinese, Whitlam allowed himself to be guided by Zhou Enlai. After all, he did not want to be presumptuous; his host was one of the most powerful people in the world and had a famously penetrating intellect. For forty-four years Zhou Enlai had been a member of the inner circle of the Chinese Communist Party – even longer than Mao.[47] The breadth and depth of his experience and knowledge was unparalleled in China. On the world stage he was feared and respected. 'His mind ranged back and forth over issues over time', Stephen FitzGerald described to me in 2011: 'He had a context for talking about international issues which was enormous. It was analytical and pretty unusual.'[48]

FitzGerald paused for a moment, and then in a soft voice he continued:

> Gough has a similar kind of mind. It was apparent to some extent in that meeting but it became more apparent when Gough became Prime Minister. If Zhou talked about great power relations going back into the forties, Gough was also with him on that instantly.[49]

Whitlam's initial discomfort quickly passed. The conversation was both a high-stakes game and a rich historical discussion. Zhou's main goal was to draw Whitlam into denouncing Australia's alliance with America under the ANZUS treaty. Several times he manoeuvred the discussion so that the two men found an area of agreement, then he would passionately assert China's view and pause to hear Whitlam's own – daring him to disagree. After exchanging pleasantries, Zhou secured confirmation of Whitlam's policy to withdraw troops from Vietnam, asking, with Taiwan and Japan in his mind, whether this extended to other countries too. Whitlam assured him that this was Labor's general policy. The Premier, satisfied, reached for his tea and turned the conversation where he wanted it to go. He brought up a statement Whitlam had made to Ji Pengfei:

> You mentioned in your discussions that you looked upon the ANZUS treaty as preventing restoration of Japanese militarism. That is a fresh approach to us.

> Whitlam: Australia has only been attacked by one country in her history – Japan. So Australians at [the time of signing the ANZUS treaty] had a fear of the Japanese. They had the same fear of the Japanese as I believe your people have now.[50]

Zhou tried to move this parallel to the present tense, but Whitlam skilfully avoided spelling out the contemporary justification for ANZUS, except to say that it was entirely defensive.[51] But, Zhou probed, 'you are also a member of SEATO. You cannot call SEATO a defensive treaty.' His announcement sparked laughter from the Chinese officials. 'This time', he continued, 'it is not a good treaty.' Whitlam responded simply: 'It is moribund.'[52] Australia's involvement in ANZUS and SEATO represented its desire to see the West in the Asia-Pacific region. The declaration that SEATO was 'moribund' was a recognition that this Western influence was on the decline.

The importance of SEATO and ANZUS to the Chinese Premier became more apparent as the talks progressed. Both had been cultivated by John Foster Dulles, the former US Secretary of State (1953–59), for whom Zhou held a strong dislike. Alongside America's 'so-called treaty' with Jiang Jieshi for the defence of

Taiwan and Quemoy, they represented what Zhou feared to be an aggressive American policy of encirclement: China's south-eastern borders were surrounded by a series of multilateral and bilateral defence pacts engineered by America. While Australia saw American involvement in Asia as imperative to its defence, China saw it as aggressive imperialism. On this revelation, one Australian journalist present remarked, rather naively:

> If his statement does no more, it should remind Australians that far from being the unpredictable monster that we have been led to believe she is, China is a country with fears, worries and foreign problems of its own.[53]

That such a basic realisation was worth spelling out is testament to the grip fearful images of China continued to have on the Australian imagination. For some, this very public conversation was an important step towards shifting Australian attitudes towards China.

The Premier again sought common ground with Whitlam, this time drawing a comparison between Australia's relationship with America and China's pact with Russia (the Sino-Soviet Friendship Treaty of Alliance and Mutual Aid). In recent years, China's dealings with its ally, the Soviet Union, had turned sour through mutual suspicion and doctrinal divergences. Zhou still felt betrayed and he warned Whitlam against trusting unreliable allies, asking: 'Is your ally very reliable?'[54] Whitlam was careful to reject the parallel: there had been no similar deterioration in relations between Australia and America. Zhou Enlai threw up his arms. 'But they both want to control others.' He beat his wicker chair for emphasis. 'Our socialist country will not be controlled by anyone.'

Zhou's deep sensitivity about China's dignity as an independent power was shared by many of the Chinese that the Australians had met. To Zhou, expansionism was a dirty word. The events of the last two centuries, since China had been dethroned by the West as the dominant world power, weighed heavily on his mind. China's recent split with the Soviet Union had only served to intensify the general distrust of Japanese militarism and American imperialism. These three powers – Russia, America and Japan – were the driving concerns of Chinese foreign policy and were regularly touted as the three international evils in the pages of the propaganda newspapers. As one Chinese official advised Whitlam on the trip, 'To understand the Chinese you must understand their history.'[55]

'Yours has been a bitter experience', Whitlam sympathised, 'and I understand your feeling.' But he warned Zhou about fearing American imperialism:

> I still deplore the destructive style of John Foster Dulles, but his soul does not keep marching today. The American people have broken President Lyndon Baines Johnson and if Richard Milhous Nixon does not continue to withdraw his forces from Vietnam they will destroy him similarly. The Australian people have had a bitter experience in going all the way with LBJ. They know America made [Prime Minister Harold Holt] change his policy and they will never again allow the American President to send [Australian] troops to another country.[56]

Within this comment we can see the signs of how Whitlam would redefine the America-Australia relationship during his Prime Ministership. His reference to Harold Holt's infamous line 'All the way with LBJ' expressed his pent-up frustration with what he perceived to be twenty-two years of Liberal governments' subservience to America. In this statement, we see his belief that Australia has its own national interests and could act independently on that basis. Indeed, we can also see the confidence with which he felt he could criticise the United States Government as an equal in the alliance.[57] Moreover, by doing this from China, he emphasised the priority he placed on developing a regionalism that was not dominated by the great powers.[58] In Australia, Whitlam was lambasted for this comment, but Zhou received it well: 'Such a very good appraisal of the American people.'[59]

The Chinese Premier stopped testing Whitlam on the question of ANZUS and instead turned to Australian domestic issues, about which he was remarkably well informed. He had evidently judged that Whitlam was a good chance to gain office in 1972 and, unlike Ji Pengfei or Bai Xiangguo, felt no delicacy was needed in discussing the policies of the McMahon Government: 'You are clear that the position of your present Australian Government is not friendly to China', he asked, 'That you are clear about?' Whitlam did not reply. He had refrained from engaging in party politics since his arrival in Hong Kong. Zhou continued, though, trying to unsettle Whitlam:

> It is probably because you have come to China to lead a delegation that the Australian Prime Minister has declared yesterday that the establishment of diplomatic relations with China is a far off thing.[60]

The clipped line from McMahon's press statement in Perth was the first news the delegation had heard from Australia since their arrival in China. It made a mockery of McMahon's publicly stated belief that China did not pay attention to statements made by 'other people'.[61] Whitlam cautiously responded:

> This may be the case – but I must say to the credit of my opponents that they are catching up with the realities of life regarding China to a certain extent. When Nixon says he wants to visit China, can McMahon be far behind?[62]

To this, Zhou Enlai laughed heartily. As Whitlam has repeated with satisfaction in the years since, 'I was not in on the joke.'[63] Few people were.

As Zhou and Whitlam conversed in the Great Hall of the People, Dr Henry Kissinger, Nixon's Assistant for National Security Affairs, was in Bangkok, supposedly on a 'world fact finding tour'. In three days time he would arrive in Islamabad, where, feigning a stomach ache, he would quietly slip off to Peking. The object of his secret mission: talk with the Chinese and lay the foundations for a visit by Nixon himself. This historic visit was very much on Zhou Enlai's mind. Whitlam had, unwittingly, made an historic in-joke.

American interlude

On Thursday 8 July, the night before the exercise in secret diplomacy was put into action, Henry Kissinger could not get to sleep. He was buzzing with a sense of excitement and anticipation. A rare feeling of insecurity overwhelmed him as he tried to imagine what lay ahead. He had never met any Chinese communists before and he was feeling apprehensive – even frightened – about 'so momentous a mission in an unknown capital'.[64] And it certainly was a momentous mission. In the midst of the Cold War, he was being sent by the President of the largest capitalist power in the world to talk with the leaders of the most populous communist power in the world. It was the culmination of two years of overtures by the Nixon administration towards China, involving relaxations of trade and travel restrictions between the two countries, and many 'back-channel' messages to Peking through CIA stations in Romania and Pakistan.

The contact through Pakistani President Yahya Khan, made in October 1970, was the first (to quote Zhou Enlai) 'that has come from a Head through a Head, to a Head!' And as such, 'great importance' was attached to it.[65] In April 1971, after a long pause, Mao Zedong responded to the Yahya contact with 'ping-pong diplomacy'. Soon after, communicating through Pakistan's embassy in Washington, the two nations organised Kissinger's visit.[66] The Americans were elated. As Nixon read the crucial message confirming the visit, Kissinger said grandly, 'This is the most important communication that has come to an American President since the end of World War II.' Later, he would push the date back to the US Civil War.[67]

After a few restless hours in bed, Kissinger had a quick breakfast and, in the dark of 4 am, equipped with a hat and sunglasses to avoid recognition, was driven in Pakistani military vehicles to Rawalpindi airport.[68] A Boeing 707 was waiting for him. On the other side of the airport, within sight of journalists and Embassy personnel, Kissinger's official aircraft remained unmoved and unused. In a few hours time, an appropriate motorcade would be leaving for the Pakistani President Yahya's retreat in the mountains with a sick Henry Kissinger allegedly aboard. The Americans and Yahya were enthralled with the 'cloak and dagger' nature of the exercise.[69] In his political memoirs, Kissinger tells with pride and intricate detail of the elaborate webs of deception he wove and of the various contingencies for which he was prepared. He delights in recounting the alarm of his Secret Service detail, 'who had not been told of my destination and who nearly had heart attacks at what they were witnessing.'[70]

When Kissinger gained his opportunity to meet with Zhou Enlai, the talks were more intense and extensive than those in the East Room on 5 July. Zhou was quick to anchor Kissinger's lofty sense of the significance of the occasion with the reminder that the Americans and the Chinese had been meeting for almost sixteen years: 'We have met 136 times, but there's still no result.' Their meetings would not be a success simply because they were official, he continued; 'it is whether there is an intention to solve problems. This is the crux.'[71] It was on this matter that McMahon's Paris dialogue had failed. For Kissinger, however, the intention was certainly there.

The talks would occupy seventeen of the forty-eight hours the American party was in Peking. It took Kissinger a while to gain momentum, but as the meetings progressed, a sense of familiarity and even companionship emerged between the two men. At first Kissinger spoke from notes, cautious not to misrepresent the agenda of his President. In his thick German accent he outlined the American views and the agenda he hoped they might discuss over the course of their talks. He approached the discussions like a broker, separating issues into categories and seeing that each was properly resolved before progressing. Zhou, on the other hand, spoke freely and without notes in his style of grand philosophical sweeps, frequent historical analysis, and attention to fine detail. He danced around topics and subtly readjusted the American agenda. But when Kissinger departed Peking on 11 July, he left with confidence and great respect for the Chinese. He deemed his visit a great success. On his return to Islamabad, he announced to the American Ambassador, Joseph Farland, 'I got everything I wanted. It was a total success on my part. I did a beautiful job.'[72] He had in his briefcase an announcement that, he felt, would set the world on a new and more peaceful historical course. Chairman Mao Zedong and President Richard Nixon would meet within eight months.

As Kissinger flew out of China on 11 July, he wrote his briefing to the President:

> I am frank to say that this visit was a very moving experience ... These forty-eight hours, and my extensive discussions with Zhou in particular, had all the flavor, texture, variety and delicacy of a Chinese banquet. Prepared from the long sweep of tradition and culture, meticulously cooked by hands of experience, and served in splendidly simple surroundings, our feast consisted of many courses, some sweet and some sour, all interrelated and forming a coherent whole. It was a

total experience, and one went away, as after all good Chinese meals, very satisfied but not at all satiated. We have laid the groundwork for you and Mao to turn a page in history. But we should have no illusions about the future. Profound differences and years of isolation yawn between us and the Chinese.[73]

As he was scrawling these words, Whitlam was in Shanghai, enjoying his own experience with Chinese food.[74] It was his fifty-fifth birthday. He was celebrating in the restaurant of the Peace Hotel, in the company of the Governor of Shanghai. After the many courses of the banquet, a cake was brought in ceremoniously, tactfully adorned with a single candle, and presented to Whitlam 'with Premier Zhou Enlai's compliments'.[75]

⚜

Back in the East Room of the Great Hall of the People on Monday 5 July, however, Whitlam did not know what the weeks before him would hold. Despite the rapidly changing international environment, few predicted the American and Chinese policy shift. The secrecy of the affair veiled it from all but a handful of officials involved; not even Nixon's White House staff knew of Kissinger's visit. But it was on Zhou Enlai's mind when talking with Whitlam. The Premier even ventured a question about Kissinger. Whitlam responded tersely that he had not met the man.

Throughout the entire conversation, Zhou did not broach the question of Taiwan, which had dominated his talks with Kissinger and which had been all important in the Australians' other discussions in Peking. Nor did Zhou raise the issue of the increasing number of US military bases on Australian soil, a matter of great concern to the Chinese.[76] His silence was taken as a good sign. 'With a man so deliberate in his mind and clear in his purposes', Whitlam would later write, 'one must place as much significance on what he omits to say as on what he does say.'[77] Zhou had conducted the meeting with Whitlam on the assumption that Australia under Labor could instate normal diplomatic relations with the PRC. This verdict was perhaps the most significant immediate outcome of the visit.

On one final point in the meeting, Whitlam pondered aloud whether, with better policies and a closer Sino-Australian relationship, the destruction and slaughter in Vietnam could have been avoided. He was cut off by Zhou, who, having run China on a day-to-day basis for more than two decades, would not accept such abstract speculation. With a grand gesture, he proclaimed 'What is past is past', before adding more encouragingly, and no doubt with McMahon's failed Paris talks in mind: 'and we look forward to when you can take office and put into effect your promises.'[78]

III

The reaction at home

'The Zhou-Whitlam debate', the journalist Bruce Grant wrote at the time, 'is one of those unexpected dramatic events that make or break political reputations because they capture the public imagination. It will become a part of Australian political folklore and Mr. Whitlam is the beneficiary.'[79] Grant's words typified the sentiment felt by those Australian journalists who had witnessed the spectacle. There was a general sense that 'Mr Whitlam [had] held his ground well in a testing situation with a brilliant political debater and negotiator.'[80] One journalist called it 'a virtuoso political performance', 'a masterpiece in diplomacy, public relations, mental agility and sheer tactics'.[81] The only Australian in the room who was perhaps a little disappointed with the meeting was Rex Patterson, who was annoyed that Whitlam had not seized the opportunity to ask the Premier about wheat.[82]

The public setting had proved ultimately to be a blessing for Whitlam, who thereafter could not be credibly accused of backroom dealings with the Chinese. They had also unexpectedly afforded him the extraordinary opportunity to display his credentials, as an Opposition Leader, on the world stage. That Whitlam had not only engaged equally with one of the world's most formidable statesmen, but even challenged Zhou Enlai on some issues, deeply impressed the accompanying journalists. Here was a leader who gave Australia international presence. One journalist stridently declared that Whitlam 'and his party have shown the way to Peking. The onus is on Mr. McMahon to pursue the dialogue and continue the initiative.'[83]

The editorials at home were mixed. Most reactions were predictably aligned with the various newspapers' political inclinations: some vigorously condemned the meeting as 'a disastrous performance', others commended the Opposition Leader for having 'behaved as a potential Prime Minister and Foreign Minister should'.[84] The Government's reaction was slower, but when it did come, it brought a tempest with it.

※※

On Monday 12 July, Prime Minister William McMahon stood in front of a thundering crowd of Young Liberals in Melbourne. 'It is time', he raged, 'to expose the shams and absurdities of [Whitlam's] excursion into instant coffee diplomacy.'[85] Applause filled his ears. Invoking Menzies' traditional rationale for the Vietnam War (to 'stop the downward thrust of China between the Pacific and Indian Oceans'), he continued, in mock disbelief:

> He went on playing his wild diplomatic game, knocking our friends one by one until he was virtually alone in Asia and the Pacific, except for the communists ... I find it incredible that at a time when Australian soldiers are still engaged

in Vietnam, the leader of the Labor Party is becoming a
spokesman for those against whom we are fighting![86]

His accusation of Whitlam's collusion with China joined a series of
criticisms directed against the Opposition Leader.[87] Whitlam's late-
night meeting with the Chinese Premier was especially ridiculed,
with McMahon declaring, as his speech reached its crescendo:

> In no time at all Zhou Enlai had Mr Whitlam on a hook and
> he played him as a fisherman plays a trout.[88]

This single line continues to echo in the halls of history. Former
diplomat Alan Renouf has argued for its place alongside Prime
Minister Harold Holt's unfortunate declaration of servility to
America: 'All the way with LBJ'.[89] Lance Barnard, Labor's deputy
parliamentary leader, discounted the criticisms 'as a by-product
of impotence, spleen and deep personal envy'.[90] Three days after
McMahon's trout speech, Nixon announced to the world the news
of Kissinger's visit.

The announcement

At 7.31 pm on 15 July 1971, President Richard Nixon broadcast live
on American radio and television from NBC studios in Burbank,
California. He spoke for three minutes, reading a statement that
was being simultaneously issued in Peking. In a serious tone, his
eyes uncomfortably flitting between his notes and the camera, he
revealed that his Assistant for National Security Affairs, Henry
Kissinger, had just returned from a secret diplomatic mission
to China. Nixon himself intended to visit Peking before May
1972. The meeting between leaders, Nixon read, 'is to seek the
normalization of relations between the two countries and also
to exchange views on questions of concern to the two sides.' He

hoped that his visit would become a 'journey for peace', stressing his 'profound conviction that all nations will gain from a reduction of tensions and a better relationship between the United States and the People's Republic of China.'[91]

The announcement rocked the international community. In China, the news was received on the ground with surprise, confusion and curiosity. Many Chinese wondered why it was that Nixon, who had been described in Peking as 'a god of plague and war', should be invited to their country.[92] A similar astonishment was felt in the political headquarters of Taipei and Seoul, but it was accompanied by unease and sparked outrage.[93] Official silence cloaked the stunned surprise of Soviet leaders. As Kissinger had predicted, the Chinese and American policy shift had sent 'enormous shock waves around the world'.[94]

The initiative was well received by most members of the American Congress, who hoped that Nixon's visit would help end the Vietnam War. Some heralded the announcement as 'an all-important turning point in America's quest for peace', 'a brilliant diplomatic initiative' and 'a further indication that he is a President who intends to solve problems, not perpetuate them'.[95] The news was applauded by many Western leaders, but none were more vocal in their support than the Canadians. Prime Minister Pierre Elliott Trudeau hailed America's policy shift as a 'bold and decisive' step towards bringing China into world affairs, while his Secretary of State for External Affairs, Mitchell Sharp, described it, with a certain satisfaction, as 'a very, very welcome development'.[96]

The news had particular and peculiar impact in Japan and Australia. Gough Whitlam, who had completed his own tour of China, heard the broadcast from Tokyo and quickly called on the Prime Minister of Japan, Eisaku Sato. With tears welling in his eyes, Sato confided to Whitlam his despair and humiliation. Through a technical glitch, he had not been informed about the change in American policy: 'The journalists told me about it.'[97]

A similar response was being stirred in Canberra, with an irate McMahon feeling embarrassed and betrayed by the initiative. He had known of the policy shift only a few hours in advance.[98] Indeed he had received a letter from President Nixon as late as 14 July, without mention of anything about China.[99] The lack of consultation made a mockery of Australia and America's 'candid' relations. Years later, McMahon recalled to Freudenberg that his 'played like a trout' speech had been checked before delivery with the American Embassy in Canberra. He added ruefully: 'I thought I was helping them.'[100]

Despite his inner turmoil, McMahon publicly welcomed the announcement of Nixon's impending visit to China, declaring to the press, somewhat dubiously, that 'normalising relations with China has been our policy for some time.'[101] Questions at the announcement were strictly forbidden. According to journalist Laurie Oakes, he appeared 'shaken and embarrassed'.[102] Barnard was less kind; continuing the piscatorial metaphor, he compared the Prime Minister to 'a stunned mullet'.[103]

Privately, however, McMahon was furious. He complained to President Nixon about Australia's 'lack of any foreknowledge of what is certainly a dramatic step in the foreign policy of the United States.' He underlined the depth of his 'quandary' by referring to the political implications of Whitlam's visit to China, and he emphasised his sense of abandonment: 'we have attempted under all circumstances to co-ordinate our policies and support you in what you are doing.' The lack of communication between the two allies, he continued uncomfortably, 'has naturally led to the assumption that our relations are not as close as they should be.'[104]

McMahon did not receive the reassurance he desired. The American Secretary of State, William Rogers, promised to keep in mind the substance of the Prime Minister's message and Nixon passed on his personal regards, but the response was overall unapologetic: 'The question of the President's visit was an exceptional one on which it had just not been possible to let many know.' Under this line, in McMahon's hand writing, is scribbled: 'But they trusted the Pakistanis!! Not us!! Or Japan!!'[105]

Minister and friend Peter Howson worried about McMahon's mood. 'The main task is for him to get some rest', Howson wrote after the two men dined on 20 July, 'he certainly looks tired and is a little tense and terse.'[106] Talking with Howson, McMahon confided that he saw the China debacle as a 'real failure' of his Prime Ministership and he stressed his frustration with Nixon's lack of consultation. Outside The Lodge, however, McMahon sought to deflect his emotional wounds onto Whitlam, announcing weakly to the Australian press: 'It makes an awful farce of Whitlam's visit. Whitlam did not even know that Kissinger was there. That's how much the Chinese trust him. It makes a mockery of the man.'[107]

Whitlam felt neither snubbed, nor mocked. He and his fellow travellers to China were euphoric. Stephen FitzGerald and the remaining members of the ALP delegation were in the Chinese city of Wuxi when they heard the news. In 2011, he described to me the reaction:

> Extraordinary vindication. I suppose we were more surprised and stunned than anything. I mean that's your initial reaction and then immediately you start to put it in context.[108]

The context was politically brilliant for Labor. As the Chinese official who broke the news cheekily commented, 'Perhaps your Prime Minister won't be talking anymore about trout.'[109]

Coda

After the talk with Zhou Enlai, Whitlam reflected most on a part of the conversation that had eluded the press. As the two men walked out of the East Room, Zhou spoke to Whitlam directly in English. 'You are very young to be the leader of a major political party', he remarked. Whitlam responded: 'I am the same age you were at Geneva', referring to the international peace conference on Indo-China in 1954.[110] Zhou paused for a moment. His mind cast back to a memorable day at the Geneva conference when he had come face-to-face with John Foster Dulles. Zhou had extended his hand, offering an international token of friendship to the American Secretary of State. Dulles refused to participate in the ritual – in some accounts he is reported as saying, 'I cannot.'[111] He put his hands behind his back, and strode out of the room. It was a potent denunciation of a leader and his people. Seventeen years later, Zhou, in a thoughtful voice conveyed the depth of the insult to the tall Australian beside him: 'You know that Foster Dulles would not even take my hand.'[112]

As Whitlam would later write, 'Nothing more poignantly sums up two decades of lost opportunities down the blind alley of the Dulles policy of containment of China.'[113] The power of the moment was not lost on Kissinger either. While the Americans and President Yahya had been captivated by the 'cops-and-robbers atmosphere' of Kissinger's visit, the Chinese, on the other hand, were 'very hurt' by the American insistence on such extreme secrecy.[114] Were American officials ashamed to be meeting with Chinese leaders, they asked.[115] Dulles' handshake snub had not been forgotten and the Chinese were wary of Kissinger affecting a similar slight with his secret diplomacy. Kissinger was quick to reassure his hosts, but it is worthwhile pursuing this line of inquiry. Why was Kissinger's visit an act of *secret* diplomacy? One American official, Marshall Green, justified it thus: had word of the visit leaked out, 'it might have raised all kinds of criticisms from the right wing of the Republican Party, not to mention deep concern in Taiwan, Japan and other countries affected.'[116] Was this what Kissinger and Nixon were worried about and trying to avoid through secrecy? If so, how are we to explain the carelessness of the official announcement of the visit, the pain felt by international leaders such as Jiang Jieshi, Sato and McMahon, and the general approval the announcement received by the American Congress?

I identify two reasons why the visit was conducted in secrecy. First, Nixon and Kissinger had a passion for privacy. 'Without secrecy', Nixon explained to his stunned colleagues on the morning he announced his impending visit, 'there is no chance of success in it.'[17] The inscrutable Kissinger, who proudly called himself 'a specialist in secret trips', elaborated: 'We kept it secret so we would not have to negotiate with *The New York Times*.'[118] It was this shared character trait – a deep distrust of bureaucrats – that would spur Nixon's dramatic undoing as President in 1974.[119]

More importantly, however, the visit was kept secret for the simple fact that American officials felt they could not trust China. Trust, Nixon hoped, would be attained through physical contact. No number of back-channel communications, positive public statements or trade relaxations could compete with 'being there', with talking face-to-face, with shaking hands.

As Kissinger rounded off his introductory remarks on his first morning of meetings with Zhou, he attempted to finish with a flourish: 'Many visitors have come to this beautiful, and to us, mysterious, land.' Zhou raised his hand to stop him. 'You will find it not mysterious', he said matter-of-factly, 'When you have become familiar with it, it will not be as mysterious as before.'[120] In his political memoirs Kissinger reflected:

> I was taken aback, but Zhou was certainly right. Our concern
> was not the bilateral issues between us – at least at first. We
> had to build confidence; to remove the mystery. This was the
> fundamental purpose with me, as was mine with him.[121]

The enduring value of Whitlam and Kissinger's daring visits to China in July 1971 is not the immediate policy shifts that resulted, although these too are significant. It was the commitment of two political groups to enter the unknown, to confront traditional fears, and to establish a relationship of trust with a long estranged people. By the time Whitlam had completed his tour of Asia and returned to Canberra, Australia's China policy had changed forever. The mystery of the Middle Kingdom was being removed; the shimmering mirage was fading away.

Right: **American President Richard Nixon escorts Australian Prime Minister William McMahon from the White House, Washington DC, 2 November 1971**

Bettman/CORBIS

Bottom: **Gough Whitlam speaking to journalists upon returning from his visit to China, July 1971**

National Library of Australia

Chapter Three

1971 and All That

Reverberations of a visit

On his return to Australia, Gough Whitlam happily declared his China mission a success:

> Whatever may be the position of the Australian Government, Australia as a nation looks less flat-footed, less ignorant, less obscurantist, less imitative in the light of the United States initiative than she would have otherwise.[1]

It was not only Australia's international image that had benefited from the China affair; Whitlam's political image had also been made over. And, as is so often the case, the figurative transformation had manifested itself in a very literal sense. Whitlam had left for China as a slick-haired and at times severe-looking politician; he came back as a soft, wavy haired, potential Prime Minister: an icon of change. The new 'fluffy look' had been achieved by accident. While in China, Whitlam had been unable to buy any of the styling cream he was accustomed to use, and without it, in the heat and humidity, his hair returned to its natural, gentler, bouffant state.[2] It was a look that would stay with him throughout his political career.

I have indulged in this anecdote because it is symbolic of the general historical treatment that Whitlam's visit to China has received. The event was certainly a story of image, but its implications extend beyond the shine it added to Whitlam's political career or how Australia appeared on the world stage. It was a pivotal moment in Australian perceptions of, and engagement with, Asia; a revealing test of Australia's alliance with the United States; and the genesis of a long and fruitful diplomatic relationship with China. Within the visit, we find the ingredients of the changes that he would institute as Prime Minister and Foreign Minister after he was elected in December 1972.

This chapter assesses the influence and aftermath of Whitlam's visit to China in 1971. First, it probes the pain that McMahon felt on the news of Nixon's 15 July broadcast, arguing that his reaction was symptomatic of a deeper trauma that gripped Australia. His moment of anguish lays bare the fragile foundations on which his Government built its foreign policy. Second, it explores Whitlam's embrace of Asia and the bitter reaction this realignment of interests drew from the United States. At this turbulent moment in the Australia-America relationship, it explores the question: what was the ANZUS alliance supposed to mean? Finally, I look to the immediate and lasting impact of Whitlam's visit to China in 1971.

I

The decline of Australia's 'great and powerful friends'

It was not wheat or ping-pong, but geographical proximity and a keen sense of inevitability that drove Whitlam to China in 1971. It was the same proximity – a fear of the 'near north' – that kept McMahon in Australia. Both men were acutely aware of Minister for External Affairs Percy Spender's axiom: 'No nation can escape its geography.'[3]

For McMahon, these words were imbued with the same sense of dread and anxiety as they were for their speaker on 9 March 1950. For Whitlam, they were words of political and economic possibility. He welcomed the notion that Australia's future belonged with its region. To understand the different geopolitical perspectives, it is imperative to explore two of the major foreign policy currents that underpinned this moment. The first is the decline of Australian ties with its 'great and powerful friends'. The second is the questioning and concern in Australia about what to do in their absence.

In the same week that Whitlam left for China, Britain finally established the terms with which it would enter the European Economic Community (EEC) in January 1973.[4] Britain's bid for full EEC membership, first put forward in 1961, was a statement to the international community that it no longer possessed the material strength or political influence to sustain an empire. The decision inspired gloom and outrage amongst Australian leaders, who feared what a downgrading of the Commonwealth might mean for their important economic, military and cultural relationship with Britain.[5] A decade later, although the shock and sense of abandonment had faded, the trauma lingered. Australia mourned its imperial past. In early June 1971, the Australian Minister for Trade and Industry, Doug Anthony, had travelled to Brussels and London to plead Australia's case for special consideration one last time.[6] His appeals fell on deaf ears. Australia was not granted trade concessions, on the basis that it was neither poor nor overwhelmingly economically dependent on Britain. It was still dependent, however, on the old certainties about Australian Britishness.

As James Curran and Stuart Ward have shown, Britain's retreat into the EEC and its withdrawal of residual military forces east of Suez, also realised in 1971, were more than just blows to Australia in terms of trade and security; they symbolically severed the familial ties between the two nations and catapulted Australia into a crisis of national meaning.[7] In the words of Prime Minister Harold Holt in 1966, Australia had been 'jolted by events to adulthood'.[8] The naming of Australia's new decimal currency in 1963,[9] the scrapping of British passports in 1967 and the demise of Empire Day and the upgrading of Australia Day, all revealed a consensus within Australia about the need to move on from the imperial past and establish a post-imperial future. But what would that future be? Nixon's recognition of defeat in Vietnam and his 1969 announcement of America's retreat from Asia – known as the Guam doctrine – made it clear that Australia could not rely on the United States to determine that future.[10] The two main pillars around which Australia built its foreign policy were crumbling. Instead of answers to the sea of questions facing them, Australians were gripped, as one commentator remarked, by 'a commendable emptiness' about their place in the world.[11] It was an emptiness that went beyond the vexing issues of nationalism and identity to raise traumatic questions about Australia's aspirations and orientations in an alien, post-imperial Asia.

These simmering anxieties reached boiling point on 15 July 1971. Despite Nixon's carefully worded warning of retreat to America's regional allies in 1969, both Gorton and McMahon had continued to view the ANZUS treaty as the backbone of Australian foreign policy. When Nixon announced his China initiative, without consulting or even properly informing the Australian Government, McMahon was forced to confront the dreaded question at the back of his mind: could Australia rely on the United States?[12] His anxiety was heightened by the fact that it was over China, Australia's psychological nemesis, that the alliance had been put under pressure. The unfamiliarity of China underlined the profound uncertainty of the new post-imperial, multi-polar world in which Australia found itself.

The aftermath: Eighteen months of tattered China policy

The unfortunate Leslie Bury, having served for four months as Australia's Foreign Minister, was the first political victim of Nixon's announcement. He was replaced in his role by Nigel Bowen, a man who would describe Australia, in a potent declaration of the Government's lack of vision or ambition in foreign affairs, as 'at present small and relatively insignificant'.[13] Despite the shock of the Nixon announcement, the McMahon Government had neither the imagination nor the courage to forge its own path on the next big China issue: the vote on recognition of the PRC at the UN. On 28 October the PRC entered the General Assembly with a resounding majority, while the nationalist regime in Taiwan was expelled.[14] Australia and America, refusing to budge from their support of a 'Two China' policy, were two of thirty-five nations who voted against the initiative. As one political commentator despaired, 'Once again Australia could be seen on the world stage following the lead of [the] US in a way which appeared to be out of touch with reality.'[15]

Edmund S.K. Fung has written in depth about the McMahon Government's continued, yet inhibited, attempts to establish a dialogue with Peking after Whitlam's visit.[16] In the eighteen months between Whitlam's visit and McMahon's defeat, Australian China policy is remarkable only for its lack of coherence. In October 1971, for example, McMahon was offered a golden opportunity to regain political initiative on China when Andrew Peacock, then Minister for the Army, was unexpectedly invited to visit Peking with the understanding that he would meet Zhou Enlai.[17] Although tempted to accept, McMahon and Bowen feared internal party criticism and, in a direct insult to the Chinese, vetoed the invitation. By the end of the year they were forced to reassess their stance on recognition and ordered the third ever review of Australian policy towards the PRC – it was also the second within twelve months.[18] The unexceptional 1972 review did not vary significantly from its predecessor, and it retained the main obstacle to recognition: Government support for a 'Two China' policy. Even when the Chinese unexpectedly renewed their Australian wheat contracts in September 1972 – a sign that they would deal with either party in government, McMahon failed to seize the opportunity to reopen the dialogue with Peking. His priorities lay elsewhere.

McMahon travelled to Washington and London in October–
November 1971, seeking assurances from Australia's traditional pro-
tectors and trading partners of their continued commitment to the
Asia-Pacific region.[19] Although he did not get the security guarantees
he wanted from London, he returned from Washington with what he
saw as an important, albeit symbolic, triumph. His bitter protests to
Nixon about the lack of consultation on the China announcement had
earned him a secret 'hot-line' between the offices of the Australian
Prime Minister and the American President.[20] The 'hot-line', which
McMahon believed to be the first of its kind, was designed so that
the leaders could communicate freely and frequently on important
issues. Its existence was to reassure Australia that the ANZUS treaty
still had substance, even if that came in the form of a telex machine
rather than unconditional military support.[21] McMahon's solution to
the uncertainties confronting Australia in a post-imperial world was
to obligate the US in any way possible to extend its Asian presence.

The 'hot-line' existed for thirteen months and was used five
times, primarily to exchange birthday wishes.[22]

II

McMahon and America: 'You are with us, come what may'

McMahon's concern about the strength of ANZUS was warranted.
The China affair was only the most recent in a series of occasions where
the United States had fallen short of fully confiding in Australia.
The asymmetry of the partnership and the relative reliability of the
relationship arguably engendered in America a certain casualness
about the alliance. It was not that Nixon had *wanted* to exclude
Australia – indeed he had often signalled the need to coordinate his
China policy with that of Australia, New Zealand and Japan – it was
just that he did not *think* of Australia at the crucial moment.[23] While

Japanese Prime Minister Sato had not been warned about the China decision because of a careless technical glitch, there was no such excuse for the Australians.[24] Nixon's slip of mind on 15 July 1971 was indicative of a deeper pattern. In 1964 one Australian complained to the US Assistant Secretary for East Asian and Pacific Affairs, William Bundy, that Britain was better informed about US dealings in North Vietnam than Australia. The response that Bundy offered was telling of the American attitude to Australia: 'We have to inform the British to keep them on side. You are with us, come what may.'[25]

McMahon was aware of this perception, but had difficulty coming to terms with it. In the 1971 Department of Foreign Affairs review of Australian China policy, which I analysed in chapter one, he resigned himself to the fact that 'we cannot expect to be kept fully informed by [America and Japan] on any moves they might make to normalise relations.'[26] Elsewhere in the same review is written: 'We can expect the Americans to keep us fully briefed on every detail of change in their position.'[27] The contradiction sums up the quandary that faced McMahon. What Whitlam dismissed as the Australian Government's 'me-too' policy on China was in fact a constant challenge to sustain.[28] This was epitomised by one recommendation McMahon put forward in the 1971 review on China policy: for Australia 'to keep one jump ahead of the United States' and set an example for Nixon.[29] Although this seems like a stunning movement away from dependence on America, it is in fact the exact opposite. McMahon saw it as a means to sustain closer ties with his 'great and powerful friend': to anticipate Nixon's next initiative so that Canberra and Washington could move together in the future as well as the present.

With his call for action on the China issue, McMahon also had on his mind the growing importance of the Asia-Pacific region in a post-imperial world. 'It does not always do our image good in Asia', he wrote in February 1971, 'to be constantly following America's lead.'[30] He recognised that it was in Australia's interests to set a more independent course of action in its region and continue the initiatives towards Asia that Harold Holt had tentatively started five years earlier.[31] But, not for the first time, this remained only a theoretical realisation. As Alison Broinowski has argued, since the early history of settler Australians, recognising Asia's importance has rarely been followed by decisive efforts to bridge the gap between East and West.[32] It was not only party disunity and disorganisation that restrained McMahon from taking the 'jump'. He could not bring himself to accept the realities of the changing international situation: he was paralysed in old thinking about China. His fear of the unfamiliar outweighed his efforts at *realpolitik*.

When world opinion dramatically changed on China with Kissinger's visit, however, he understood its significance and desperately sought to claim some of the credit. Calling upon the failed Paris dialogue as his evidence, he rewrote history, declaring that 'we haven't, as it were, been forced by ping-pong diplomacy to take the kind of action recently taken.'[33] Indeed he was audacious enough to later decree that he had started 'a new epoch for Australia'.[34] Whitlam, less dubiously, also asserted his stake in the bipartisan Australian policy shift towards normalising relations with China. The picture he painted of the international situation was that of leaders like Canadian Prime Minister Pierre Elliott Trudeau and, to a much lesser extent, himself, showing the Australian and United States' Governments the path to Peking. It was not the first time he fancied himself as leading the US on the question of China.[35] And it would certainly not be the last. Whitlam's strides towards Asia independently of America would ruffle more than a few feathers in Washington when he assumed office.

Whitlam and America: 'Great and powerful associates'

'The general direction of my thinking is towards a more independent Australian stance in international affairs', Whitlam announced at his first press conference after being sworn in as Prime Minister.[36] On his first day in office he enacted this independent approach, continuing the style of diplomacy he had showcased with his visit to China. Within weeks he had called for neutrality in the Indian Ocean, stopped aid to Vietnam, and conducted full discussions with China and countries throughout South East Asia – all without consulting America. Once more the question arose: what does the Australia-America alliance mean? But this time it was the Americans who were doing the asking.

In late December Whitlam sent Nixon a letter of reproach for the recent bombings of Hanoi and Haiphong, decreeing that the US cannot rely on Australia always and unconditionally.[37] American officials were incensed.[38] The main insult, Kissinger later described to the Australian Ambassador, was that Whitlam had treated America as if it were 'on a par with other foreign countries'.[39] The turbulent start to the relationship was compounded by what Alan Bloomfield and Kim Richard Nossal have described as a pronounced 'anti-Americanism' within the Labor Party. Some of Whitlam's ministers, most notably Jim Cairns, Clyde Cameron and Tom Uren, called the Nixon administration, respectively, 'corrupt', 'maniacs', and, with Nixon and Kissinger in mind, 'mass murderers'.[40] The 'very bad feeling' Whitlam had caused in America was all the more profound, Kissinger explained, 'because the President has a warm spot towards Australia.'[41]

This 'warm spot' explains much about the ANZUS treaty. Unlike most international bilateral relationships, the Australian-American alliance took its cue less from geopolitical or economic interests than from the similarity and compatibility of language, culture and values.[42] Nixon's 'warm spot' was similar to McMahon's Americaphilia: both were products of familiarity. The strains Whitlam caused on the relationship were not the result of any anti-Americanism – indeed he viewed ANZUS as the only 'perfect' alliance.[43] They came about because, as Prime Minister, he rejected sentimentalism and tried to sculpt a new relationship with America. Although his 'independent' foreign policy continued to function within the existing framework of Australia's all-important security and trade relationships with America and Britain, there was a change in the tone of the relationship.[44] McMahon's 'great and powerful friend' became Whitlam's 'great and powerful associate'.[45]

Ironically, as the warm feeling between Australia and America declined, the consultation process was forced to improve.[46] Washington recognised the need to work harder with Canberra to maintain the high standard of their relations. Instead of arranging a telex machine for Australia, Nixon sent the highly regarded diplomat, Marshall Green, to serve in Canberra.[47] It was one sign of the new respect Americans were according to their old ally and it demonstrated an effort on Nixon's part to consolidate his 'warm spot'.[48] After all, it was not only Australia that was forced to reassess its place in the world at the time – Nixon and Kissinger were extremely wary of the new fluidity in international affairs, and they also knew that détente was inherently fragile. Familiarity was a rare commodity in an increasingly multipolar world, and they worked to sustain it. Whitlam, on the other hand, needed to change the tone of the Australia-America relationship. With the transformation from 'friend' to 'associate', he created rhetorical space for the unfamiliar in Australia's external relations. It was a statement that geography and economics, not history or culture, would be the driving factors in Australia's relations with the world. For Whitlam's foreign policy vision, America and Britain had to be on the same playing field as China and Japan.

III

Recasting the relationship with Asia: An assessment of the visit

In a recent survey of the Australian Parliament (2010), Deng Xiaoping's decision in 1978 to liberalise the Chinese economy was singled out as having the greatest influence on the character of contemporary

Australia-China relations.[49] The second most popular historical mile-stone was the extension of political recognition to the communist government of China by Australia in December 1972. The visit to China by Whitlam in July 1971 did not make the cut. It was not even included as an option in the survey. Why has this moment been passed over? For a nation emerging from the imperial embrace, trying to find its feet in a foreign region and desperate for clear markers of maturity, why is this visit not enshrined in the national consciousness as a decisive act of independence in international relations?

Perhaps the answer lies in the partisan nature of the enterprise, something that Deng Xiaoping's decision certainly cannot be accused of. Perhaps it is because Whitlam was an Opposition Leader at the time, giving the visit an unofficial element. Or perhaps it is because the 1972 act of diplomatic recognition, the Whitlam initiative that flowed on from the visit, is regularly celebrated.[50] These three reasons explain why the 1971 visit was not included in the parliamentary survey, but they are no justification for this event to be so consistently breezed over in Australian political history.[51]

The immediate benefits emerging from the ALP visit to China were threefold. First, Whitlam, in his talks with Chinese officials, had confirmed the terms on which Australia could establish a diplomatic relationship with the PRC: the Canada formula. It was this groundwork that enabled him to extend political recognition as soon as his Government gained office.[52] Second, it forced the issue of recognition into public debate, exposing the incoherence of McMahon's China policy, and emphasising the need for an independent and imaginative Australian foreign policy. The third is what Whitlam called the 'symbolic significance' of the visit.[53] This was not a political or domestic symbolism, as foreign affairs rarely featured as an election issue. In Whitlam's eyes, the visit stridently announced to Australia's neighbours and allies that a new government would 'mean a clear change and new initiatives in Australian foreign policy'.[54] It signposted the watershed in Australia's external relations that would come under a Whitlam Government.

The visit had longer-term impacts, too. On the human level, it laid the foundations for Australia to confront the practical challenges of managing an asymmetrical and cumbersome relationship.[55] The contacts made on that trip would form the framework of the Australia-China partnership for decades to come. Stephen FitzGerald, the young advisor and interpreter to the delegation, became the first Australian Ambassador to China. Like Frederic Eggleston in Chungking, FitzGerald's enthusiasm, intelligence and energy, in the words of Australian historian Geoffrey Blainey, 'did wonders for our name and our relation'.[56] But the influence of the visit in July 1971 worked both ways. One of the delegation's hosts, Hua Jundo, was later appointed an ambassador to Australia. 'He and Gough in their later years often joked and reminisced about the fact that he had been Gough's translator', FitzGerald related to me in 2011.[57] Another host, Hu Hongfan, also continued contacts with Australia through his role as an Ambassador in Papua New Guinea, while Bai Xiangguo visited Australia in July 1973, on the two-year anniversary of Whitlam's first visit to China.

The most significant impact of the events of July 1971, however, was the immediacy with which China lurched into Australian consciousness. One member of the ALP delegation, Graham Freudenberg, later stressed the improbability of the whole enterprise:

> If a fortune-teller had told me at the beginning of 1971 that I would go either to China or the moon that year, I would probably have opted for the moon as the more probable destination.[58]

By the end of the year, the Leader of the Australian Opposition had visited China and the Prime Minister was giving it serious thought. (Soon after Nixon announced that he was visiting Peking, McMahon privately inquired whether he might be able to accompany him![59]) By March 1972 McMahon had revealed publicly that, with the right circumstances, he would think to visit China.

Ten years later, Australia was the number one source of tourists to China on a per capita basis. Fifty-three thousand Australians were travelling to the moon each year.[60]

⚘

When Whitlam returned to Peking as Prime Minister on 31 October 1973, the carnival-like atmosphere he encountered was nothing like the late-night, informal reception of two years earlier. A military procession heralded his arrival, followed by a precisely choreographed dance performance. Seven thousand children waving streamers of pinks and greens and reds and yellows cheered and sang 'warm welcome' in Chinese to the Australians as they emerged from the plane. On the tarmac, there to greet Gough and Margaret Whitlam personally, stood Zhou Enlai. Whitlam was clearly moved by the reception. The two leaders stood side by side as an Australian flag was raised to a rendition of 'Advance Australia Fair'. Later, as the official group made their way to their sleek black cars, the familiar melodies of 'Click go the Shears' and 'Waltzing Matilda' blared through the airport loudspeakers. Whitlam described his return trip as a 'sentimental as well as a diplomatic journey'; he saw it as a fulfilment of the promises he had made to Zhou Enlai in 1971.[61]

Over the course of his four-day visit, Whitlam spent seventeen hours in conversation with Zhou Enlai, and he was even granted an hour-long meeting with the ailing Chinese leader, Mao Zedong. The visit coincided with the largest bilateral sugar agreement ever signed between the two countries and a significant three-year wheat contract.[62] The reception could not have been warmer and at the closing banquet on the evening of 3 November, Whitlam and Zhou spoke about the new level of 'friendship' Australia and China shared. Whitlam, in his last overseas speech as Foreign Minister, declared the misunderstandings of the past generation to be over: 'I deeply regret that Australia was so slow in reaching friendship with China, but I may say on behalf of my people and nation, that once we make a friend, we are unshakeable and unswerving in that friendship.'[63]

Whitlam was true to his word. He would make the journey to China nine more times over the next thirty years, becoming a vital and respected pillar of the Sino-Australian relationship. And, importantly, his successor, Liberal Prime Minister Malcolm Fraser, normalised Whitlam's actions. In a dramatic change of custom, Fraser made his first international calls as Prime Minister not to London or Washington, as was tradition, but to Peking and Tokyo.[64] It gave the Australia-China relationship a bipartisan endorsement, and symbolically consolidated Australia's new orientation towards Asia. Fraser's influence is not to be underestimated. He not only maintained the relationship, thus assuring longevity for Whitlam's legacy, but he built upon it. And he did so for very different reasons. Unlike Whitlam, who developed the relationship thinking of a new regionalism for Australia in the Asia-Pacific, Fraser was primarily interested in how the Chinese could be used to counter Soviet hegemony. He saw a good relationship with China as crucial to ending the Cold War, and his strong anti-Soviet views made him popular with the Chinese.[65] Among other initiatives, he regularised reciprocal visits by politicians, officials and business people to China, established educational exchanges, and increased cultural ties.[66]

The forty years since Whitlam's first visit to China have been transformative for the Sino-Australian relationship. China has moved rapidly from the periphery of Australia's foreign policy vision to the centre.[67] In June 1971, only one Member of Parliament, Charles Griffiths, had ever been to China. Bob Hawke, in his private and public career, has now made the journey more than eighty times.[68] And in 2003, Prime Minister John Howard took the relationship to a new level, inviting President Hu Jintao to become the first non-American foreign head of state to address Australian Parliament.[69]

Today the Asia-Pacific region buys 70 percent of Australia's exports. China alone is responsible for more than a third of that trade.[70] How much of this was a result of the reorientation towards Asia engineered by Whitlam? Gareth Evans and Bruce Grant have described the Whitlam era in foreign policy as 'a meteorite, short and dramatic, rather than a star, stable and lasting'.[71] They argue that while Whitlam shattered the past patterns of Australian foreign policy with his focus on regionalism and international-ism over the traditional alliances, his tenure as Prime Minister was too short for him to craft a new course for Australia. Graham Freudenberg holds a contrary view. He contends that Whitlam's initiatives in Asia, although products of their time, continued to set the pattern of Australian foreign policy for the next decade.[72] I am inclined to settle somewhere in between. As Nancy Viviani argues, the significance of Whitlam's embrace of Asia was that he 'changed Australians' perceptions and attitudes, which allowed his successors to carry out their policies.'[73] On no policy is this clearer than China. When Whitlam left Australia on Sunday 27 June 1971, China was a forbidding unknown in Australia, more the product of fantasy than a viable destination. When he flew back into Australia on Saturday 24 July 1971, the debate on China had irrevocably changed.

Not only was there bipartisan agreement that Australia should normalise relations with the PRC, but it had become something of a political priority. This change of tone rang clear in McMahon's 28 July announcement that the Australian Government had 'no hostility to the great Chinese people whose history and culture have contributed much to the achievements of mankind.'[74] The diplomacy of the ALP visit had forced political movement, while its sense of drama and adventure captured the public imagination. Across Australia there were those, like thirteen year-old Kevin Rudd, who began to think about China in a different way. Of course, long-established images do not change overnight, or in the space of a month, or a year. But, as Alison Broinowski and Anthony Millar remind us, 'Perceptions are powerful in the way societies respond to each other.'[75] Even the smallest shift can have long and lasting influence. The China breakthrough continues to reverberate today.

Gough Whitlam listens at the Echo Wall in the Temple of Heaven in Peking, November 1973

The acoustics of the smooth, circular wall allows even a whisper to carry a long distance.

National Archives of Australia

Epilogue

It is 10.40 am on 16 January 1973 and a small crowd of journalists and Australian officials are huddled beside the customs hall in Hong Kong, watching earnestly as a gaunt figure stumbles his way across the Lo Wu Bridge from mainland China. An old grubby grey suit hangs from the skeletal frame and a mop of unruly short hair crowns his head. This unkempt and unshaven man is Francis James. The fifty-four year old Australian journalist is walking to freedom, having spent the last 1169 days imprisoned by the Chinese under the charge of espionage. His body weak from hunger and fatigue, he leans on the frame of the Australian Commissioner, Ivor Bowden, beside him. In an unprecedented move by Chinese officials, Bowden has been allowed entry into Chinese territory to help James make the crossing. It is a small flourish to the 'friendly gesture' of James' release. We are witnessing a defining moment in the new relations between the Australians and Chinese, a moment which has its seeds in the ALP visit to China, eighteen months previously. James and Bowden reach the small welcome committee. The activity of his release and the exhaustion of three long, hard years in prison are too much for James. He collapses. A helicopter is at bay and he is soon swept off to hospital.[1]

✣

Throughout the visit to China in 1971, Francis James was on Gough Whitlam's mind. The two men had attended Canberra Grammar School together. When news came through of James' disappearance in China in November 1969, Whitlam followed his case with interest. In June 1969 London's *The Sunday Times* had published James' slightly elaborated description of a visit to several secret Chinese military and industrial complexes. The article did not have a good reception in China; it was accused of being 'a complete fabrication'. Only a few months later, in October, James returned to China.[2] He was last seen by a German businessman leaving on the train from Canton to Hong Kong on 4 November. After that, there was only silence.[3]

Some of Whitlam's staff, including his Press Secretary Richard Hall, assumed the rumours of James' arrest were true and became members of the Australian Francis James Freedom Committee. Whitlam was urged to broach the matter with the Chinese while in Peking. And so he did. As accompanying journalist Laurie Oakes writes, during the visit 'Mr. Whitlam worked for Mr. James' release.'[4] At every opportunity he discretely asked Chinese Officials for news on the imprisoned Australian journalist. The response was always the same: 'We have no knowledge of this matter.' At the end of the trip, on a train ride from Canton to Hong Kong, the ALP's principal guide sat next to Whitlam and quietly relayed three messages: 'Your friend is in China. He is well. He has broken China's laws.'[5] This was the first news of James since his disappearance in 1969.

This train-ride exchange of information is important. It demonstrates a level of respect by Chinese officials for the delegation and an effort on their part to foster friendly relations. Whitlam comprehended the significance of the message and treated the issue delicately, not raising the matter publicly, but staying in close contact with James' family.[6] Soon after his return, he wrote to Zhou Enlai personally, explaining that James was a friend of his and a friend of China. He attached copies of James' articles advocating political recognition and withdrawal of troops from Vietnam.[7] The contact worked.

But when news got through to Australian officials, McMahon and Bowen sought to gain political capital out of the event: they did not want Whitlam to get the domestic credit. In April 1972 James was driven to the Hong Kong border to be released, but when the

Chinese saw ambulances and medicos on the other side, they turned away, insulted. James was driven in a Chinese military vehicle back to his small, rectangular prison cell.[8] The Government's assertion, however true, that the Chinese had mistreated the Australian journalist, resulted in James serving another nine months in prison.

The Australian Government's mistake was in maintaining the mirage of China; viewing it as a political card, not a country; thinking domestically, not internationally. McMahon was still functioning under the publicly stated belief that 'China has always served the Liberals well politically and will continue to do so.'[9] Whitlam's visit to China in 1971 challenged this view. It was a significant step away from the insular and highly imaginative perspective of China in Australian politics. It was a significant step towards a more engaged and open-minded treatment of China in Australian domestic debate and international affairs. When James walked free on 16 January 1973, it was the product of this new style of diplomacy and was helped by the channels of communication that were simultaneously being established at the Australian Embassy in Peking.

The relationship between Australia and China remains cross-cultural. Contact requires delicacy, understanding and, to some extent, trust. Eleven years after James was released, all charges of espionage against him were dropped and the flamboyant Australian journalist was officially invited to return to China. The action was testament to the strong cultural bridge that a small delegation of Australians had carefully begun constructing in July 1971.

Notes

Front matter

'You have had many barbarian invasions, but I am not sure that you are prepared for this one.'

– Henry Kissinger, US Assistant for National Security Affairs, to Chinese Premier Zhou Enlai, Peking, 11 July 1971. Memcon, Henry Kissinger and Zhou Enlai, 11 Jul 1971, 10:35–11:55 am, in William Burr, ed., 'National Security Archive Electronic Briefing Book No. 66: September 1970–July 1971', *The National Security Archive*, 27 Feb 2002 [online] at: http://www.gwu.edu/~nsarchiv/NSAEBB/NSAEBB66/#docs, accessed 4 Aug 2011, document 38, p. 5.

[1]   Christopher I. Beckwith, *Empires of the Silk Road: A History of Central Eurasia from the Bronze Age to the Present* (Princeton: Princeton University Press, 2009), pp. 320–362, esp. 358–361.

Introduction

[1]   Gough Whitlam, *The Whitlam Government 1972–1975* (Ringwood, Victoria: Viking, 1985), pp. 12–24; Laurie Oakes, *Whitlam P.M.* (Sydney: Angus and Robertson, 1973), p. 234.

[2]   Bill Hayden, *Hayden: An Autobiography* (Sydney: Angus & Robertson, 1996), pp. 156–57.

[3]   Jenny Hocking, 'Post-War Reconstruction and the New World Order: The Origins of Gough Whitlam's Democratic Citizen', *Australian Journal of Politics & History* 53:2 (2007), pp. 223–235, 232.

[4]   David Marr, 'We need to talk about Kevin … Rudd that is', *The Sydney Morning Herald*, 7 Jun 2010.

5   See, for example, Kevin Rudd, 'Foreword: The Road to China', in Gough Whitlam, *The Road to China* (Hong Kong: Cosmos Books, 2010), pp. 5–6. In another report he recalled a non-existent 1972 visit to China by Whitlam, see Kate Hannon, 'Whitlam Joint Legacy Honoured', *The Canberra Times*, 29 Apr 2007.

6   Here are three examples of volumes that rush over the visit in a *single sentence* when one might expect more thorough coverage: James Walter, *The Leader: A Political Biography of Gough Whitlam* (St Lucia, QLD: University of Queensland Press, 1980), p. 66; T.B. Millar, *Australia in Peace and War: External Relations 1788–1977* (Canberra, Australian National University Press, 1978), p. 292; Lachlan Strahan, *Australia's China: Changing Perceptions from the 1930s to the 1990s* (Melbourne: University of Cambridge Press, 1996), p. 278. There are volumes that give the visit serious, albeit passing, attention. Most notably David Goldsworthy et al, 'Reorientation', in David Goldsworthy, ed., *Facing North: A Century of Australian Engagement with Asia, Volume 1: 1901 to the 1970s* (Melbourne: Melbourne University Press, 2001), pp. 310–371, esp. 329–338.

7   The sheer quantity of factual errors in the literature is astounding; I offer here three examples. A small portrait of the visit originally published in *The Monthly* includes errors such as the length of time the ALP was in Opposition, the content of the correspondence between Whitlam and Zhou Enlai, the time of the meeting between the two men, the date of Whitlam's birthday and the date of Whitlam's second visit to China, see Shane Maloney and Chris Grosz, *Australian Encounters* (Melbourne: Black Inc., 2010), pp. 34–35; basic errors such as the date of the delegation's arrival in Hong Kong and the date of Nixon's announcement can be found in Jenny Hocking, *Gough Whitlam: A Moment in History* (Melbourne: Melbourne University Press, 2008), pp. 377, 380 (Hocking creates a misleading timeline by merging two of McMahon's speeches); and errors regarding the number of accompanying journalists and the details of the telegram inviting Whitlam to China are reproduced in Brian Carroll, *Whitlam* (Kenthurst, NSW: Rosenberg Publishing Pty

Ltd, 2011), pp. 70–73. Even the National Archives of Australia has published grossly incorrect information about the visit. See for example National Archives of Australia, 'Timeline: Gough Whitlam', *Australia's Prime Ministers* [online] at: http://primeministers.naa.gov.au/timeline/results.aspx?type=pm&pm=Gough%20Whitlam, accessed 2 Sep 2011.

8   Some of this information can be found in the Personal Papers of Richard Hall, Gough Whitlam and Graham Freudenberg. The closest thing on the public record to a complete itinerary of the whole visit was scrawled in Freudenberg's rough handwriting on a scrap of paper from the Peking Hotel, see National Archives of Australia (NAA) (Sydney), M156, 25, 'Personal Papers of Prime Minister E.G. Whitlam', G. Freudenberg (personal), Box 2, 'Peking Hotel, China', undated.

9   George Megalogenis' book, *The Australian Moment*, is a welcome exception. Megalogenis identifies Whitlam's relationship with China, along with his tariff reform, as the two Whitlam initiatives that, to paraphrase his subtitle, 'made us for our times'. George Megalogenis, *The Australian Moment: How we were made for these times* (Camberwell, Victoria: Viking, 2012), pp. 16–17, 36–37, 345.

10   Stephen FitzGerald, *Talking with China: The Australian Labor Party visit and Peking's foreign policy* (Canberra: Australian National University Press, 1972).

11   'Barbarians in the Middle Kingdom' and the 'Shimmering Mirage' are both phrases coined by Terrill. Ross Terrill, *800,000,000: The Real China* (London: Heinemann, 1972). The book's initial version, as an article in the *Atlantic Monthly*, was the first thing Henry Kissinger gave President Richard Nixon to read in preparation for his 1972 visit to Peking. See Arthur Waldron, 'Friendship Reconsidered', *Taiwan Review*, 4 Jan 1993 [online] at: http://taiwanreview.nat.gov.tw/ct.asp?xItem=99296&CtNode=1347, accessed 6 Jun 2011.

12   See, for example, Graham Freudenberg, *A Certain Grandeur* (Camberwell, Victoria: Viking, 2009); Graham Freudenberg, *A Figure of Speech: A Political Memoir* (Milton, QLD: Wiley, 2005); Laurie Oakes, *Whitlam*

P.M.; Laurie Oakes and David Solomon, *The Making of An Australian Prime Minister* (St. Kilda, Melbourne: *Cheshire Publishing Pty Ltd*, 1973).

13 A recent collection of Whitlam's speeches, *The Road to China*, offers important insight into his analysis of the visit and of the Sino-Australian relationship.

14 R.G. Collingwood, *An Autobiography* (London: Oxford University Press, 1939), p. 110.

15 NAA (Sydney), C475, ARCH 99F/0368, 'Various segments – moving images', 2–7 Jul 1971, program NPZ628/VISP1925.

16 Edmund S.K. Fung and Colin Mackerras, *From Fear to Friendship: Australia's Policies towards the People's Republic of China* (St Lucia, QLD: University of Queensland Press, 1985), esp. 109–111; Edmund S. K. Fung, 'Australia's China Policy in Tatters 1971–72', *The Australian Journal of Chinese Affairs* 10 (Jul., 1983), pp. 39–59; Roderic Pitty, 'Way behind in following the USA over China: The Lack of any Liberal Tradition in Australian Foreign Policy, 1970–72', *Australian Journal of Politics and History* 51:3 (2005), pp. 440–450; Neville Meaney, 'The United States' in W.J. Hudson, ed., *Australia in World Affairs, 1971–75* (Sydney: George Allen & Unwin, 1980), pp. 163–208.

Chapter One: The Shimmering Mirage

1 Ross Terrill, *800,000,000*, p. 12.

2 Although Jenny Hocking and Graham Freudenberg record that the delegation left Australia on 28 June, Freudenberg in fact arrived in Hong Kong on 26 June and the rest of the official delegation followed on 27 June. See NAA (Canberra), A1838, 3107/38/12/7 PART 1, 'ALP Delegation 1971 (1)', Letter from J.R. Burgess to R.H. Robertson, Hong Kong, 29 Jun 1971.

3 NAA, 'ALP Delegation 1971 (1)', Inward cablegram to the Department of Foreign Affairs from Australian Trade Commission in Hong Kong, 2 Jul 1971.

4   Rex Patterson was the uncertainty. Freudenberg, *A Certain Grandeur*, p. 209.

5   Anon., 'Press agony over China', *The Review*, 4 Jul 1971; NAA, 'ALP Delegation 1971 (1)', Reuters telegram, 2 Jul 1971.

6   NAA, 'ALP Delegation 1971 (1)', Outward cablegram from the Department of External Affairs to the Australian Trade Commission in Hong Kong, 23 Jun 1971.

7   E.M. Andrews, 'Australia and China, 1949: The Failure to Recognise the PRC', *The Australian Journal of Chinese Affairs* 13 (Jan 1985), pp. 29–50; Henry S. Albinski, *Australian Policies and Attitudes Toward China* (Princeton, New Jersey: Princeton University Press, 1965), pp. 26–27.

8   Britain was not alone; twelve other countries effected immediate recognition of communist China. Its reasons for recognition were first, that Peking governed mainland China, and second, that Western non-recognition could push the PRC to the Soviet Union. Alan Renouf, *The Frightened Country* (Melbourne: MacMillan Company, 1979), p. 283.

9   Eggleston as quoted in Keith Waller, *A Diplomatic Life: Some Memories*, Australians in Asia Series No. 6 (Nathan, Queensland: Griffith University Press, 1990), p. 15.

10   Frederic Eggleston, *Diaries 1941–1946*, [microform] Series 9, Items 376–1425 at the National Library of Australia (NLA), Bib ID 2090183, mfm G 24016–24018, Prose Diary, pp. 3, 88.

11   See Neville Meaney, 'Frederic Eggleston on International Relations and Australia's Role in the World', *Australian Journal of Politics & History* 51:3 (2005), pp. 359–371.

12   This is not to say, however, that Australia did not make any independent foreign policy decisions before 1940. See Neville Meaney, 'Australia and the World', in Neville Meaney, ed., *Under New Heavens: Cultural Transmission and the Making of Australia* (Sydney: Heinemann Educational Australia, 1989), pp. 379–450, 417.

13   Waller, *A Diplomatic Life*, p. 9.

[14] Warren G. Osmond, *Frederic Eggleston: An intellectual in Australian Politics* (Sydney: Allen & Unwin, 1985), pp. 215, 227, 233.

[15] See Albinski, *Australian Policies and Attitudes Toward China*, pp. 5–12.

[16] Eggleston, *Diaries 1941–1946*, 6 Oct 1942.

[17] Richard White, 'Australian journalists, travel writing and China: James Hingston, the "Vagabond" and G.E. Morrison', *Journal of Australian Studies* 32:2 (2008), pp. 237–250, 239.

[18] Though Eggleston was not without his own orientalist traits. See Strahan, *Australia's China*, pp. 34–36; David Walker and John Ingleson, 'The Impact of Asia', in Meaney, *Under New Heavens*, pp. 287–324, esp. 309–315.

[19] Eggleston, *Diaries 1941–1946*, 3 Jan 1943.

[20] P.D. Phillips, 'War Trends in Australian Opinions' in Australian Institute of International Affairs, *Australia and the Pacific* (Princeton: Princeton University Press, 1944), p. 68.

[21] Eggleston, *Diaries 1941–1946*, 30 Oct 1941.

[22] In this context Australia has been called 'An Anxious Nation' and 'A Frightened Country'. See David Walker, *Anxious Nation: Australia and the Rise of Asia 1850–1939* (St Lucia, QLD: University of Queensland Press, 1999); Renouf, *The Frightened Country*.

[23] A recent study that ranges from 1972 to 2010 argues that Australian foreign policy continues to be defined by ambivalence, between seeing Asia as a sign of fear and hope. See Carol Johnson et al, 'Australia's Ambivalent Re-imagining of Asia', *Australian Journal of Political Science*, 45:1 (Feb 2010), pp. 59–74.

[24] H.V. Evatt, *Current Notes on International Affairs* 20 (Oct 1949), pp. 1084–1085.

[25] Henry S. Albinski, 'Australia and the China Problem Under the Labor Government', *Australian Journal of Politics & History* 10:2 (Aug 1964), pp. 149–172, 170; Timothy Kendall, *Within China's Orbit? China*

through the Eyes of the Australian Parliament (Canberra: Department of Parliamentary Services, Parliament of Australia, 2008).

26 See Stuart Doran and David Lee, eds., *Documents on Australian Foreign Policy: Australia and Recognition of the People's Republic of China, 1949–1972* (Canberra: Department for Foreign Affairs, 2002).

27 Spender in a letter to Lester Pearson, the Canadian secretary of state for External Affairs, 2 Mar 1950, as quoted in Andrews, 'Australia and China, 1949', p. 36.

28 Cablegram to New York, For Spender only from Menzies, Canberra, 21 Oct 1950, document 21, in in Doran and Lee, *Australia and Recognition of the People's Republic of China, 1949–1972*, pp. 28–29.

29 Meaney, 'Australia and the World', pp. 415–421.

30 NAA, 'Australia/China Relations – policy', Percy Spender, 'Relationship between Australia and China', For Cabinet, Canberra, 19 Feb 1951.

31 There is no evidence in the documents, but it has been suggested that such a conversation took place when John Foster Dulles visited Canberra in 1951. See, for example, John Burton, *The alternative: a dynamic approach to our relations with Asia* (Sydney: Morgans Publications, 1954), p. 91. This claim has been refuted in Alan Watt, *The Evolution of Australian Foreign Policy 1938–1965* (London: Cambridge University Press, 1967), pp. 240–243. Both Albinski and Andrews offer good synthesis of the issue, see Albinski, *Australian Policies and Attitudes Toward China*, pp. 106–107; Andrews, 'Australia and China, 1949', pp. 37–38.

32 Roger Bell, 'The American Influence', in Meaney, *Under New Heavens*, pp. 325–377, 360–362.

33 As quoted in NAA (Canberra), A1838, 3107/38/20 PART 2, 'Cabinet Papers on Policy, 1971–1980', William McMahon, 'Australia's policy towards China', Department of External Affairs, 9 Feb 1971, p. 18.

34 C.P. Fitzgerald, 'China, Korea and Indo-China', in Gordon Greenwood, ed., *Australian Policies Toward Asia: Part VI* (Melbourne: Australian Institute of International Affairs, 1954), p. 5.

35   David I. Kertzer, *Ritual, Politics, and Power* (New Haven: Yale University Press, 1988), p. 2.

36   The literature is vast. See for example Walker, *Anxious Nation*; Alison Broinowski, *The Yellow Lady: Australian Impressions of Asia* (Melbourne: Oxford University Press, 1992), esp. pp. 6–13.

37   Eric Rolls, *Sojourners: The epic story of China's centuries-old relationship with Australia* (St Lucia, QLD: University of Queensland Press, 1992), p. 456.

38   Ibid., pp. 18–19.

39   Though it is worth remembering that this was not one stream of legislation leading to the White Australia policy; most of the 1850s legislation was repealed in the 1860s. Meaney, 'Australia and the World',p. 386.

40   R.G. Menzies, 'International Affairs', House of Representatives, *Debates*, 5 Aug 1954, pp. 65–66.

41   Hugh Leslie, 'International Affairs', House of Representatives, *Debates*, 12 Aug 1954, pp. 276–278, 277.

42   Hocking, *Gough Whitlam*, p. 153.

43   James Curran, *The Power of Speech: Australian Prime Ministers Defining the National Image* (Melbourne: Melbourne University Press, 2004), pp. 83–87.

44   Stephen FitzGerald, Personal Communication, 16 Aug 2011.

45   Gough Whitlam, 'International Affairs', House of Representatives, *Debates*, 12 Aug 1954, pp. 272–276, 273, 275.

46   Whitlam maintained a remarkably consistent policy on China since he first publicly supported recognition in 1954. See, for example, E.G. Whitlam, 'What Should Australia's Foreign Policy Be?', 23 Jan 1961, University of Western Australia, *Whitlam Institute e-collection*; E.G. Whitlam, 'Australian Foreign Policy 1963', 9 Jul 1963, The Australian Institute of International Affairs, *Whitlam Institute e-collection*; E.G. Whitlam, 'Australia – Base or Bridge?', 16 Sep 1966, University of Sydney, *Whitlam Institute e-collection*.

47   In 1951 Chifley described the United Nations refusal to admit the PRC as a member state as 'the greatest diplomatic folly I knew of'. Ben Chifley, 'International Affairs', House of Representatives, *Debates*, 7 Mar 1951, p. 85.

48   H.V. Evatt, speaking on 20 March 1955 after the traumatic Hobart conference, as quoted in Robert Murray, *The Split: Australian Labor in the Fifties* (Melbourne: Cheshire, 1970), pp. 232–233.

49   Ibid., p. 252.

50   Murray, *The Split*; I.F.H. Wilson, 'China' in Hudson, *Australia in World Affairs, 1971–75*, pp. 271–282, 272–273.

51   I am indebted to an anonymous referee for stressing the significance of the DLP's role in shaping Australian political perspectives of China.

52   P.L. Reynolds, *The Democratic Labor Party* (Melbourne: The Jacaranda Press, 1974), pp. 33–34.

53   Renouf, *The Frightened Country*, p. 277.

54   Gregory Clark, *In Fear of China* (Melbourne: Lansdowne, 1967), pp. 169–172.

55   R.G. Menzies, 'Vietnam–Ministerial Statement', House of Representatives, *Debates*, 29 Apr 1965, pp.1060–1.

56   NAA (Sydney), M170, 70/141, Set 1, Box 1, 'Personal Papers of Prime Minister E.G. Whitlam', E.G. Whitlam, 'Australia and China', Article for Community Aid Abroad Journal 'Now', 16 Dec 1970.

57   Gough Whitlam, 'My Mission to China', *The Australian*, 4 Jul 1971, p. 2.

58   As quoted in James C. Thomson, Jr., 'On the Making of U. S. China Policy, 1961–9: A Study in Bureaucratic Politics', *The China Quarterly* 50 (Apr–Jun 1972),pp. 220–243, 241.

59   Britain Foreign Papers (Marlborough, England: Adam Matthew Digital, c2010), FO 371/186997, Political relations: Australia in Great Britain, Foreign Office files for China, 1949–1980. Section III, 1967–1980, A.J. de la Mare reporting on conversation with the leader (G.A. Jockel) of

an Australian delegation from the Department of External Affairs to London, 'Australia and the Hard Line', 11 Oct 1966.

[60] Gary Klintworth, *Australia's Taiwan Policy 1942–1992*, (Canberra: Australian Foreign Policy Papers, The Australian National University, 1993), p. 45; Joel Atkinson, 'Australian Support for an Independent Taiwan Prior to the Recognition of the People's Republic of China', *Australian Journal of Politics & History* 57:1 (2011), pp. 68–85, 79.

[61] This argument is put forward in E.M. Andrews, *Australia and China: The Ambiguous Relationship* (Melbourne: Melbourne University Press, 1985), p. 193; Goldsworthy et al, 'Reorientation', p. 330.

[62] Britain Foreign Papers, A.J. de la Mare, 'Australia and the Hard Line', 11 Oct 1966.

[63] Ibid.

[64] Richard M. Nixon, 'Asia after Viet Nam', *Foreign Affairs* 46 (1967–68), pp. 111–125.

[65] The overt initiatives began in July 1969 with a relaxation of restrictions on trade and travel. This was followed in December the same year and in April 1970 with further relaxations of the trade embargo and in January 1971 with the exchange of scientific information between the United States and China. Robert S. Ross, *Negotiating cooperation: the United States and China, 1969–1989* (Stanford: Stanford University Press, 1995), pp. 17–54.

[66] Pitty, 'Way behind in following the USA over China'.

[67] H.V. Evatt, 'International Affairs', House of Representatives, *Debates*, 16 Mar 1950, p. 919.

[68] Lindsay Barrett, *The Prime Minister's Christmas Card: Blue Poles and cultural politics in the Whitlam era* (Sydney: Power Publications, 2001), pp. 66–67.

[69] One cause of the wheat trade is far from flattering for Australia. As one Chinese trade official explained, the poor quality of Australian wheat

made it suitable to mix with the even poorer quality Chinese wheat. Terrill, *800,000,000*, p. 177.

[70] This was, however, only an assertion. In 1967, for example, Australia twice used the wheat trade for political purposes. First, the Australian Security Intelligence Organisation capitalised on the access allowed to the Australian Wheat Board to bug the Bank of China in Hong Kong. Later in the year Australian officials threatened China that they would suspend the supply of wheat if the Chinese Government did not call off the riots in Hong Kong. (A rather baffling use of power considering the British described the riots as locally generated.) FitzGerald, *Talking with China*, p. 13.

[71] NAA, 'Australian wheat sales on credit to mainland China', C.F. Aderman, 'Mainland China – wheat negotiations', For Cabinet, Canberra, 10 Mar 1966.

[72] Feng-hwa Mah, 'Comment: Why China Imports Wheat', *The China Quarterly* 48 (Oct–Dec 1971), pp. 738–740, 740; Ramon H. Myers, 'Wheat in China – Past, Present and Future', *The China Quarterly* 74 (Jun 1978), pp. 297–333.

[73] Ross Terrill, 'Australia and China', *Nation*, 7 Aug 1971, pp. 12–14, 13.

[74] J. L. Granatstein and Robert Bothwell, *Pirouette: Pierre Trudeau and Canadian Foreign Policy* (Toronto: University of Toronto Press, 1990), pp. 178–189; Arthur E. Blanchette, *Canadian foreign policy, 1945–2000: major documents and speeches* (Kemptville, Canada: The Golden Dog Press, 2000), pp. 136–141.

[75] NAA, 'ALP Delegation 1971 (1)', Inward cablegram from the Australian Trade Commission in Hong Kong to the Department of Foreign Affairs, 5 Jul 1971; John R. Walker, 'China to buy more wheat', *The Montreal Gazette*, 7 Jul 1971, p. 21; Anon., 'Well done, Mr. Pepin', *The Montreal Gazette*, 6 Jul 1971, p. 6.

[76] Jonathan D. Pollack, 'The Opening to America', in Denis Crispin Twitchett and John King Fairbank, eds., *The Cambridge history of China*,

Volume 1 (Melbourne: University of Cambridge Press, 1991), pp. 402–474, 402–407; Dwight H. Perkins, 'China's economic policy and performance', in ibid., pp. 475–539, 480–494.

77   Stephen FitzGerald, 'China in the Next Decade: An End to Isolation?', *Australian Journal of Politics & History* 17:1 (Apr 1971), pp. 33–43; Anon., 'Restoration of International Ties', *Asian Recorder*, 16–22 Jul 1971, pp. 10258–10259.

78   NAA, McMahon, 'Australia's policy towards China', 9 Feb 1971, pp. 20, 21.

79   Bill Hayden, 'Australia's China Policy Under Labor', *The Australian Journal of Chinese Affairs* 11 (Jan 1984), pp. 83–97, 84–85.

80   NAA, McMahon, 'Australia's policy towards China', 9 Feb 1971, p. 19.

81   This was in part to keep pace with a review ordered by Nixon. U.S. Department of State: Office of the Historian, Foreign Relations of the United States, 1967–1976, Volume XVII, China, 1969–1972, Document 97, National Security Study Memorandum 106, Henry A. Kissinger, 'China Policy', Washington, 19 Nov 1970.

82   Roderic Pitty, David Goldsworthy and Stephen FitzGerald have been quick to stress that this review was presented by the Department of Foreign Affairs *to* McMahon for consideration, not developed *by* McMahon himself. However, given that he ordered, edited and added to the document, and then presented it to Cabinet as Foreign Minister, I attribute full authorship to McMahon. See Pitty, 'Way behind in following the USA over China', pp. 446–447; Goldsworthy et al, 'Reorientation', p. 333–334; Stephen FitzGerald, 'Australia's China Problem: Self-Imposed Isolation', *Meanjin Quarterly* 30:2 (Jun 1971), pp. 191–204, 191.

83   NAA, McMahon, 'Australia's policy towards China', 9 Feb 1971, p. 74, 33, 76, 79, 71.

84   Ibid., pp. 71, 76.

85   Indeed there had been a mini-exodus of China-watchers from the Department in the late 1960s for this very reason. Ann Kent, 'Australia-China Relations, 1966–1996: A Critical Overview', *Australian Journal of Politics and History* 42:3 (Aug 1996), pp. 365–84, 367.

86   Bob Howard, 'Foreign Policy Review', *The Australian Quarterly* 43:3 (Sep 1971), pp. 97–108, 99.

87   Broinowski, *The Yellow Lady*, p. 198.

88   Anon., 'Australian Table Tennis Delegation Visits China', *Peking Review*, 7 May 1971, p. 30; Clark, 'Chapter 7a', *Life Story*.

89   Fourth, if you count John McEwen's caretaker Prime Ministership of 19 December 1967 to 10 January 1968. R.F.L. Smith, 'Political Review', *The Australian Quarterly* 43:2 (Jun 1971), pp. 110–120.

90   Henry S. Albinski, *Australian External Policy Under Labour* (University of Queensland Press, Brisbane, 1977), p. 36; Julian Leeser, 'Sir William McMahon (1908–1988)', Australian Dictionary of Biography, forthcoming.

91   Peter Sekuless, 'Sir William McMahon', in Michelle Grattan, ed., *Australian Prime Ministers* (Chatswood, NSW: New Holland Publishers, 2010), pp. 312–323, 321.

92   Peter Golding, *Black Jack McEwen: Political Gladiator* (Melbourne: Melbourne University Press, 1996), pp. 180–82.

93   Peter Howson (ed. Don Aitkin), *The Howson Diaries: The Life of Politics* (Ringwood, VIC: The Viking Press, 1984), 6 Jan 1972, p. 813.

94   Peter Sekuless, 'Sir William McMahon', in Michelle Grattan, ed., *Australian Prime Ministers* (Chatswood, NSW: New Holland Publishers, 2010), pp. 312–323, 321.

95   Whitlam, *The Whitlam Government 1972–1975*, p. 55.

96   Outward Cablegram from Gough Whitlam to Premier Zhou Enlai, Peking, China, 14 Apr 1971, in NLA, Richard Hall Papers, MS8725, Box 51, Series 15, Folder 2.

97 Brief for Australian Delegation to the Geneva Conference, Canberra, undated, document 45, in Doran and Lee, *Australia and Recognition of the People's Republic of China, 1949–1972*, pp. 79–82.

98 NAA (Canberra), M170, 71/31, 'Personal Papers of Prime Minister E.G. Whitlam', E.G. Whitlam, 'President Nixon on China', Statement by the leader of the Opposition, Adelaide, 15 Apr 1971.

99 FitzGerald, 'Australia's China Problem', pp. 191–204.

100 Fung, 'Australia's China Policy in Tatters 1971–72', pp. 42–43.

101 The highest DLP vote was 11.11 per cent at the 1970 half-senate elections, which brought the number of DLP senators to five. Reynolds, *The Democratic Labor Party*, pp. 37–39.

102 Whitlam wanted no association with the unofficial Chinese consul in Australia: Melbourne lawyer Ted Hill. David Solomon, 'ALP Boat to China hits Stormy Seas', *The Canberra Times*, 25 May 1971.

103 Ross Terrill letter to Richard Hall, undated (c. 28 Apr 1971), in NLA, Richard Hall Papers, 51/12/2; Ross Terrill letter to Richard Hall, 28 Apr 1971, in NLA, Richard Hall Papers, 51/12/2; Etienne M. Manac'h, *La Chine* (Paris: Librairie Arthème Fayard, 1980), p. 382.

104 Ross Terrill letter to E.M. Manac'h, 28 Apr 1971, in NLA, Richard Hall Papers, 51/12/2.

105 Manac'h, *La Chine*, p. 383; E.M. Manac'h telegram to Ross Terrill, 10 May 1971, in NLA, Richard Hall Papers, 51/12/2.

106 As reprinted in Mick Young telegram to Clyde Cameron 12 May 1971, in NLA, Clyde Cameron Papers, MS4614, Box 5, Folder 1; E.G. Whitlam, Press Release, 'Proposed Visit to China – 1971', 11 May 1971, *Whitlam Institute e-collection*.

107 Oakes and Solomon, *The Making of An Australian Prime Minister*, p. 27; As corroborated in Freudenberg, *A Certain Grandeur*, pp. 208–09.

108 FitzGerald, *Talking with China*, p. 11.

[109] As quoted in Kenneth Randall, 'Cable from Peking Embarrasses McMahon: Whitlam Going to China', *The Australian*, 12 May 1971. For a more thorough announcement of his views see NAA (Canberra), A1838, 3107/38/3 PART 7, 'China – Relations with Australia, 1971–72', McMahon to Citizens Club Dinner, Sydney, 13 May 1971.

[110] NAA, 'Cabinet Papers on Policy, 1971–1980', Nigel Bowen, 'China Policy: Information Paper', Department of Foreign Affairs, 17 Feb 1972, p. 16.

[111] As quoted in Anon., 'Labor team off to China', *The Age*, 28 Jun 1971.

[112] Whitlam as reported in NAA, Reuters telegram, 2 Jul 1971.

[113] NAA, 'ALP Delegation 1971 (1)', Reuters telegram, 3 Jul 1971.

[114] Paraphrasing Whitlam as quoted in Anon., 'Labor's Five Leave for China Visit', *The Australian*, 28 Jun 1971.

[115] NAA, Reuters telegram, 2 Jul 1971; NAA, 'Various segments – moving images', 2–7 Jul 1971, program NPZ628/VISP1925.

[116] This closely mirrors a description by Ross Terrill, who travelled on this train only two weeks earlier. See Terrill, *800,000,000*, p. 1.

[117] Anon., 'Ducking Off to Peking', *The Canberra Times*, 17 Jun 1971.

[118] Eric Walsh (News Ltd), Allan Barnes (The Age), David Barnett (Australian Associated Press), Laurie Oakes (Herald and Weekly Times), John Stubbs (Sydney Morning Herald), Kenneth Randall (The Australian), Willie Phua (ABC Soundman), Philip Koch (ABC Correspondent) and Derek McKendry (ABC Cameraman).

[119] Kenneth Randall, 'Open Door to Peking', *The Australian*, 2 Jul 1971; Anon., 'Labor's China visitors ready', *The Sydney Morning Herald*, 4 Jul 1971, p. 2.

[120] Ibid.

[121] NAA, Reuters telegram, 2 Jul 1971; NAA, 'Various segments – moving images', 2–7 Jul 1971, program NPZ628/VISP1925.

[122] Interview with Tom Burns by Geraldine Doogue, 'Whitlam and China', created 8 Jul 2006, *ABC Radio National: Saturday Extra* [online] at: http://www.abc.net.au/rn/saturdayextra/stories/2006/ 1680612.htm, accessed 4 Apr 2011.

[123] Terrill, *800,000,000*, p. 2.

Chapter Two: Barbarians in the Middle Kingdom

[1] Tagline of Rolls, *Sojourners*.

[2] In November 1970 the General Assembly voted 51 to 49 in favour of seating the PRC and expelling Taiwan. A two-thirds majority, however, was needed before admission.

[3] Anon., 'Restoration of International Ties'; Anon., 'Quarterly Chronicle and Documentation', *The China Quarterly* 48 (Oct–Dec 1971), pp. 783–817; Terrill, *800,000,000*, p. 141; more generally, FitzGerald, 'China in the Next Decade', pp. 33–43.

[4] Henry Kissinger, *The White House Years* (Sydney: Hodder and Stoughton, 1979), p. 713.

[5] Joseph Camilleri, 'Foreign Policy', in Allan Patience and Brian Head, eds., *From Whitlam to Fraser: Reform and Reaction in Australian Politics* (Melbourne: Oxford University Press, 1979), esp. pp. 255–259.

[6] Whitlam, *The Whitlam Government*, p. 1.

[7] Kenneth Randall, 'A hug and an apology in Peking', *The Australian*, 9 Jul 1971.

[8] Connie Sweeris (as told to Tony Dokoupil), 'From Ping-Pong To Pyongyang', *Newsweek*, 10 Mar 2008.

[9] Gough Whitlam, 'Dateline: Peking', *The Australian*, 11 Jul 1971, p. 11.

[10] Gough Whitlam, 'Foreword', in Georg Gerster et al, *Over China* (North Ryde, NSW: Angus & Robertson Publishers, 1988), pp. 15–16, 15.

[11] Their hosts were octogenarian and President of the Peoples Institute Chang Hsi-jo, Chou Chiu-yeh, Wang Hsiao-yi, Li Shu-ten, Hu Hung-

fan, and Wei Chien-yeh. See NAA, 'ALP Delegation 1971 (1)', Telegram from the Australian Trade Commission to Leslie Bury, Hong Kong, 5 Jul 1971.

12   Freudenberg, *A Certain Grandeur*, p. 209.

13   Terrill, *800,000,000*, p. 183.

14   John Stubbs, 'Recognition Bid', *The Sydney Morning Herald*, 5 Jul 1971, p. 1.

15   For the exchange between Canberra and Paris see Cablegram to Paris; For Renouf, Canberra, 1 Jul 1971; Cablegram to Canberra, Paris, 2 Jul 1971, documents 201–202, in Doran and Lee, *Australia and Recognition of the People's Republic of China, 1949–1972*, pp. 483–486.

16   Renouf, *The Frightened Country*, p. 328; NAA, Bowen, 'China Policy: Information Paper', 17 Feb 1972, p. 16; NAA, 'Cabinet Papers on Policy, 1971–1980', M.J. Wilson, 'China: Briefing Material', 26 Oct 1971, 4(a).

17   Anon., 'No Common Sense by Peking, Says PM', *The Sydney Morning Herald*, 5 Jul 1971, p. 1.

18   NAA (Canberra), M170, 71/85, 'Personal Papers of Prime Minister E.G. Whitlam', E.G. Whitlam, 'The United States, China and Japan: Australia's Role', Speech to the Institute of International Affairs, Townsville, 25 Sep 1971.

19   They did more than this. 'Official communist sources' deliberately revealed to a journalist in Hong Kong that the Australian Maoists had tried and failed to stop Peking from receiving the ALP delegation. Perhaps, speculates Ross Terrill, Peking was irritated that Ted Hill should claim a monopoly on channels between China and Australia. Terrill, *800,000,000*, p. 184.

20   Whitlam, 'Dateline: Peking'.

21   On the first morning, after Whitlam had set the agenda for most of the session, Ji Pengfei had even asked if the delegation would agree to extend the talks into the afternoon. FitzGerald, *Talking with China*, p. 33.

22 Gough Whitlam, 'The Great Wall of China', Sydney, 27 Sep 2006, in Whitlam, *The Road to China*, pp. 22–28, 24.

23 Stephen FitzGerald, Personal Communication, 16 Aug 2011.

24 Whitlam, *The Whitlam Government*, p. 55.

25 Terrill, *800,000,000*, p. 183.

26 These words come from a talk given by Freudenberg at the Kingscliff Rotary Club, NAA (Sydney), M156, 25, 'Personal Papers of Prime Minister E.G. Whitlam', G. Freudenberg (personal), Box 2, newspaper clipping (unspecified), 'Rotary Club guest Press secretary', 13 Jan 1972.

27 Stephen FitzGerald, An ANU Convocation luncheon address given on the subject of China, 1 Dec 1976, [sound recording] at NLA, Bib ID 428102.

28 Ross Terrill, New York Times Commission, Draft to Richard Hall, undated, in NLA, Richard Hall Papers, 51/15/2.

29 Terrill, *800,000,000*, p. 180.

30 Terrill, 'Australia and China', p. 13.

31 For the experience of the ABC News team on the 1971 visit see Bob Wurth, *Capturing Asia: An ABC Cameraman's Journey Through Momentous Events and Turbulent History* (Sydney: Harper Collins Publishers, 2010), pp. 135–144.

32 NAA, 'Various segments – moving images', 2–7 Jul 1971, program NPZ639; program NPZ641.

33 Anon., 'Dr Patterson sounds out China export hopes', *Canberra News*, 7 Jul 1971.

34 On Thursday 8 July, for example, the delegation dined with the French Ambassador who helped secure their invitation to China. See Manac'h, *La Chine*, pp. 420–421.

35 Stephen FitzGerald, 'The Bogey-Man Vanishes', *The Far Eastern Economic Review*, 11 Sep 1971, pp. 32–34, 23.

36 FitzGerald, *Talking with China*, p. 17.

37 Freudenberg, *A Certain Grandeur*, p. 210; Terrill, *800,000,000*, p. 131.

38 Allan Barnes, 'Battle of wits in Great Hall of the People', *The Age*, 7 Jul 1971, p. 1.

39 John Stubbs, 'Whitlam and Chou argue on US pact', *The Sydney Morning Herald*, 7 Jul 1971, p. 1.

40 Allan Barnes, 'Centre-stage with the maestro', *The Age*, 12 Jan 1976, p. 7. Unbeknownst to the Australians, Zhou was making a habit of holding such interviews with the press, giving, for example, a recent Vietnamese delegation the same treatment. FitzGerald, *Talking with China*, p. 33.

41 Stephen FitzGerald, 'Impressions of China's New Diplomacy: The Australian Experience', *The China Quarterly* 48 (Oct–Dec 1971), pp. 670–676.

42 Whitlam, *The Whitlam Government*, p. 56.

43 These numbers are approximate. Graham Freudenberg talks of 'nearly sixty' people in the room. Freudenberg, *A Certain Grandeur*, p. 210.

44 FitzGerald, 'Impressions of China's New Diplomacy'; Stephen FitzGerald, *China and the World* (Canberra: Contemporary China Centre in association with Australian University Press, 1977), esp. pp. 88–108; FitzGerald, *Talking with China*, pp. 45–52. For a modern twist on this view of world politics see Parag Khanna, *The Second World: How Emerging Powers are Redefining Global Competition in the Twenty-first Century* (London: Penguin Books, 2008).

45 Ronald C. Keith, *The Diplomacy of Zhou Enlai* (London: The MacMillan Press, 1989), pp. 181–186.

46 Drawing, in part, from Henry Kissinger's description. Kissinger to Nixon, 'My Talks with Zhou Enlai,' 14 Jul 1971, in Burr, ed., 'National Security Archive Electronic Briefing Book No. 66', document 40, p. 7.

47 Keith, *The Diplomacy of Zhou Enlai*.

48 Stephen FitzGerald, Personal Communication, 16 Aug 2011.

49 Ibid.

50   David Barnett provided the delegation and accompanying press with an almost complete transcript of the interview in the Great Hall of the People. Barnett's original transcript can be found at NAA, 'ALP Delegation 1971 (2)', David Barnett, 'China Talk with Chou', Peking, 5 Jul 1971, but important additions, variations and details are recorded in NAA, 'ALP Delegation 1971 (2)', T.Y. Liu, 'Report on tape of conversation between Chou En-lai, his interpreter and Mr. G. Whitlam', 7 Sep 1971; FitzGerald, *Talking with China*, pp. 32–40; Terrill, *800,000,000*, pp. 15, 131–140; NAA, 'Various segments – moving images', Whitlam in China with Chou, program NPZ634. The transcript compiled from these sources is hereafter footnoted as: Whitlam and Zhou, Great Hall of the People, 5 Jul 1971.

51   The Australian Government abhorred the suggestion of a parallel, calling it 'damaging' and 'a gross misrepresentation'; see NAA, 'China – Relations with Australia, 1971–72', Dr Graeme Starr (Senior Liberal Research Officer), 'The Australian Government's views on China', 15 Jul 1971, p. 10.

52   Whitlam and Zhou, Great Hall of the People, 5 Jul 1971.

53   Anon., 'Dialogue in Peking', *The Age*, 7 Jul 1971, p. 9.

54   Whitlam and Zhou, Great Hall of the People, 5 Jul 1971.

55   Gough Whitlam, 'China and the U.S'., *The Australian*, 18 Jul 1971, p. 15.

56   Whitlam and Zhou, Great Hall of the People, 5 Jul 1971.

57   For a rapid overview of this change in Australia's treatment of the alliance, see Gareth Evans and Bruce Grant, *Australian Foreign Relations: In the World of the 1990s* (Melbourne: Melbourne University Press, second edition 1995), pp. 25–28.

58   Nancy Viviani, 'The Whitlam Government's Policy Towards Asia' in David Lee and Christopher Waters, *Evatt to Evans: The Labor Tradition in Australian Foreign Policy* (Sydney: Allen & Unwin, 1997), pp. 99–109.

59   For the outraged reaction of the Australian Government see NAA, Starr, 'The Australian Government's views on China', 15 Jul 1971, p. 10.

60   Whitlam and Zhou, Great Hall of the People, 5 Jul 1971.

61 As quoted in FitzGerald, *Talking with China*, p. 14; Taiwan, too, was keeping a close eye on Australian domestic politics at this time. See Anon., 'Timeline', *Free China Review* 21:8 (Aug 1971), pp. 45–48.

62 Tom Burns was less cautious, interjecting for the only time in the night with the comment: 'He will not be there next election'. Whitlam and Zhou, Great Hall of the People, 5 Jul 1971.

63 Whitlam, 'The Proper Course of Business with China Benefits All', p. 106.

64 Kissinger, *The White House Years*, p. 740; according to Yahya Khan, Kissinger even asked the president of Pakistan to accompany him on the mission. Margaret MacMillan, *Nixon and Mao: the week that changed the world* (New York: Random House, 2007), p. 190.

65 As quoted in MacMillan, *Nixon and Mao*, p. 175; this quote has also been attributed to Kissinger in John H. Holdridge, 'Through China's back door' in Marshall Green et al, *War and Peace with China: First hand experiences in the foreign service of the United States* (Maryland: DACOR Press, 1994), p. 116.

66 The affair is documented in dramatic detail in Kissinger, *The White House Years*, pp. 698–732.

67 As quoted in MacMillan, *Nixon and Mao*, p. 183.

68 He was accompanied by John Holdridge, Winston Lord, Dick Smyser and two secret service agents.

69 These are Kissinger's words. In a briefing he later wrote to Nixon, he joked in poor taste: 'Yahya hasn't had such fun since the last Hindu massacre!' See Memorandum for the President's Files, 'Briefing of the White House Staff on the July 15', 19 Jul 1971, in Burr, 'National Security Archive Electronic Briefing Book No. 66', document 41, p. 6.

40 Kissinger, *The White House Years*, pp. 741–742.

71 Memcon, Henry Kissinger and Zhou Enlai, 9 Jul 1971, 4:35–11:20 pm, in Burr, ed., 'National Security Archive Electronic Briefing Book No. 66, document 34, p. 7.

100 | *The China Breakthrough*

72 | Interview with Joseph S. Farland by Charles Stuart Kennedy, 31 Jan 2003, *The Association for Diplomatic Studies and Training, Foreign Affairs Oral History Project* [online] at: http://frontiers.loc.gov/service/mss/mssmisc /mfdip/2005%20txt%20files/2004 far02.txt, accessed 5 Aug 2011.

73 | Kissinger to Nixon, 'My Talks with Zhou Enlai,' 14 Jul 1971, p. 26.

74 | Freudenberg makes this link in *A Figure of Speech*, p. 127.

75 | Gough Whitlam, 'The Real Value of My First Visit to China', Crown Casino Palladium, 9 Dec 2002, in Whitlam, *The Road to China*, pp. 7–13, 11; John Stubbs, 'A memorable birthday', *The Sydney Morning Herald*, 13 Jul 1971, p. 7.

76 | For discussion of these bases in the early 1970s and their international implications, see Wayne Reynolds, 'Labor Tradition, Global Shifts and the Foreign Policy of the Whitlam Government', in Lee et al, *Evatt to Evans*, pp. 110–130, esp. 122–124; Meaney, 'United States', pp. 190–198.

77 | Whitlam, 'Dateline: Peking'.

78 | Whitlam and Zhou, Great Hall of the People, 5 Jul 1971. The Australian Government labelled this as an 'arrogant interference in Australian politics', see NAA, Starr, 'The Australian Government's views on China', 15 Jul 1971, p. 11.

79 | Bruce Grant, 'Whitlam did himself proud', *The Age*, 8 Jul 1971.

80 | Stubbs, 'Whitlam and Chou argue on US pact'. The one real embarrassment Whitlam created for himself concerned not China, but the Philippines, which Whitlam visited on his return from China. In the high pressure meeting with Zhou he alleged that Thailand and the Philippines were 'trying to insinuate themselves into China's good graces'. Whitlam and Zhou, Great Hall of the People, 5 Jul 1971.

81 | Barnes, 'Battle of wits in Great Hall of the People'.

82 | Oakes, *Whitlam P.M.*, p. 223.

83 | Anon., 'Dialogue in Peking'.

84 Quotes from editorials in the *Mercury* and the *Age*, both on 7 Jul, as quoted in C.A.H, 'Australian Political Chronicle May–August 1971', *The Australian Journal of Politics & History* 17:3 (Dec 1971), pp. 416–428, 424.

85 As quoted in Neville Meaney, ed., *Australia and the world: a documentary history from the 1870s to the 1970s*, (Melbourne: Longman Cheshire, 1985), document 389, pp. 728–730; Anon., 'Whitlam Used By Chou—PM', *The Age*, 13 Jul 1971, p. 1; John O Farrell, 'Chou had Whitlam on a hook, says PM', *The Sydney Morning Herald*, 13 Jul 1971, p. 1.

86 Ibid.

87 See, for example, Anon., 'Santamaria: Whitlam Chinese candidate', *The Sydney Morning Herald*, 12 Jul 1971, p. 2.

88 McMahon's denunciation of Whitlam was probably heightened by an exchange between the two men days earlier. Whitlam had sent him a personal cable from Peking about the latest North Vietnamese proposals, advising that they represented an 'honourable opportunity for disengagement' for the United States. In McMahon's eyes, not only was Whitlam, as Opposition Leader, engaging independently in Australian affairs abroad, but he also had the temerity to offer advice on these matters to the Australian Prime Minister! He passed the message on to American officials without comment. NAA, 'ALP Delegation 1971 (1)', Outward cablegram from the Department of External Affairs to the Australian Embassy in Paris, 10 Jul 1971; C.A.H, 'Australian Political Chronicle May–August 1971', p. 424.

89 Renouf, *The Frightened Country*, p. 330.

90 C.A.H, 'Australian Political Chronicle May–August 1971', p. 424.

91 Full broadcast published in Anon., 'President R. Nixon Plans Visit', *Asian Recorder*, 6–12 Aug 1971, pp. 10292–10293; for the drafting of the announcement see Memcon, Kissinger and Ye Jianying, 11 Jul 1971, 12–1.40 am, 9.50–10.35 am, in Burr, 'National Security Archive Electronic Briefing Book No. 66, document 37.

92 Ross Terrill, 'Nixon Visit Has Chinese Both Curious and Confused', *The Tuscaloosa News*, 23 Jul 1971, p. 14.

93   Frank Starr, 'Praise Nixon's China Visit', *Chicago Tribune*, 17 Jul 1971, p. 1; Anon., 'Dismay in Taiwan: Tokyo Welcomes Plan', *The New York Times*, 17 Jul 1971, p. 1; Anon., 'Taiwan Lodges a Protest', *The New York Times*, 16 Jul 1971, p. 1.

94   Kissinger scrawled these words in a report for Nixon as he was flying out of China. Kissinger, *The White House Years*, p. 754.

95   Senator Robert Byrd, Senator Margaret Chase Smith, Senator Robert Dole, chairman of the republican National Committee as quoted in Philip Warden, 'Called Astute Political Move: Congress Hails Nixon's Plans to Visit China', *The Chicago Tribune*, 17 Jul 1971, p. 1. An array of less favourable responses can be found at Jeffrey Hart, 'Conservatives Riled By Nixon China Policy', *The Evening Independent*, 28 Jul 1971, p. 12.

96   Anon., 'Trudeau Commends Nixon's "Bold" Step', *The New York Times*, 17 Jul 1971, p. 2.

97   Nobutoshi Nagano, *A Study of the Foreign Relations* (Tokyo: Simul Press, 1975), pp. 4–5; Osamu Miyagawa, *The impact of the Nixon shock on Japanese foreign policy toward China and Japanese economic policy* (Texas: Texas Tech University, 1987), pp. 21–33; Freudenberg, *A Certain Grandeur*, p. 216; NAA, 'ALP delegation to China 1971 (2)', Memcon, Sato and Whitlam, Tokyo, 21 Jul 1971.

98   Cablegram to Canberra, Emergency, For Prime Minister from Plimsoll, Washington, 15 Jul 1971, document 209, in Doran and Lee, *Australia and Recognition of the People's Republic of China, 1949–1972*, p. 502.

99   NAA, 'Cabinet Papers on Policy, 1971–1980', Cabinet Minute, 'Without Submission – President Nixon – Visit to China', Canberra, 20 Jul 1971.

100 Freudenberg, *A Certain Grandeur*, p. 216; Gough Whitlam, 'Human Rights: Problem of Selective Memories', Sydney, 11 Dec 1997, in Whitlam, *The Road to China*, pp. 179–194, 185.

101 Anon., 'Nixon Breakthrough', *The Australian*, 17 Jul 1971, p. 1.

102 Oakes, *Whitlam P.M.*, p. 225.

[103] C.A.H, 'Australian Political Chronicle May–August 1971', p. 425.

[104] Cablegram to Washington, For Nixon c/o Plimsoll from McMahon, Canberra, 18 Jul 1971, document 213, in Doran and Lee, *Australia and Recognition of the People's Republic of China, 1949–1972*, pp. 509–510.

[105] NAA (Canberra), A1838, 3107/38/18, 'China – Review of policy' xix, Cablegram to Canberra, 'Top Secret Immediate', Washington, 19 Jul 1971; handwriting confirmed in Doran and Lee, *Australia and Recognition of the People's Republic of China, 1949–1972*, p. 513.

[106] Howson, *The Howson Diaries*, 16 Jul, 20 Jul 1971, pp. 750–51.

[107] Anon., 'P.M. says: it's also our policy', *The Sydney Morning Herald*, 17 Jul 1971, p. 1.

[108] Stephen FitzGerald, Personal Communication, 16 Aug 2011.

[109] Gough Whitlam, 'The Proper Course for Business with China Benefits All', Beijing, 29 Jul 2002, in Whitlam, *The Road to China*, pp. 100–109, 107.

[110] Whitlam, *The Whitlam Government*, p. 57.

[111] Terrill, *800,000,000*, p. 137.

[112] Whitlam, *The Whitlam Government*, p. 57.

[113] Gough Whitlam, 'A Memorable Night 31 Years Ago', Shanghai, 2 Aug 2002, in Whitlam, *The Road to China*, pp. 57–65, 61.

[114] Although they did do their utmost to maintain Kissinger's high standards of secrecy. Kissinger, *The White House Years*, pp. 739, 740.

[115] Kissinger to Nixon, 'My Talks with Zhou Enlai,' 14 Jul 1971, p. 2.

[116] Marshall Green, 'Omens of Change', in Green et al, *War and Peace with China*, p. 92.

[117] Memorandum for the President's Files, 'Briefing of the White House Staff on the July 15', 19 Jul 1971, p. 1.

[118] Memcon, Kissinger and Zhou, 9 Jul 1971, 4:35–11:20 pm, p. 17; Memorandum for the President's Files, 'Briefing of the White House

Staff on the July 15', p. 4; 'He's a guy who believes that if you want to get things done you've got to keep them secret,' said one of the small but growing group of former associates. 'He doesn't trust the bureaucracy to keep things quiet.' Anon., 'The Inscrutable Occidental: Henry Alfred Kissinger', *The New York Times*, 17 Jul 1971, p. 2.

[119] Carl Bernstein and Bob Woodward, *All the president's men* (New York: Simon and Schuster, 1974); Bob Woodward and Carl Bernstein, *The final days* (New York: Simon and Schuster, 1976).

[120] Memcon, Kissinger and Zhou, 9 Jul 1971, 4:35–11:20 pm, p. 6.

[121] Kissinger, *The White House Years*, p. 746.

Chapter Three: 1971 and All That

[1] NAA, Whitlam, 'The United States, China and Japan: Australia's Role', p. 3.

[2] Laurie Oakes et al, *Whitlam and Frost* (Kent Town, SA: Sundial Publications, 1974), pp. 49–50; Oakes, *Whitlam P.M.*, p. 228.

[3] Percy Spender, 'International Affairs', House of Representatives, *Debates*, 9 Mar 1950, p. 628.

[4] The terms for British entry to the EEC were finally agreed to on 23 June 1971.

[5] Stuart Ward, *Australia and the British Embrace: The Demise of the Imperial Ideal* (Melbourne: Melbourne University Press, 2001), esp. pp. 88–95, 205–214.

[6] Howard, 'Foreign Policy Review', pp. 105–107.

[7] James Curran and Stuart Ward, *The Unknown Nation* (Melbourne: Melbourne University Press, 2010).

[8] As quoted in Curran, *The Power of Speech*, p. 52.

[9] I refer to the controversy that surrounded the naming of the new decimal currency in 1963. Robert Menzies' initial choice – 'the royal' – was almost unanimously criticised for its antiquated imperial origins. The name

had been selected from a number of sources, including a public naming competition, and had won out over suggestions such as the tasman, the regal, the austral, the koala, the matilda, the austbrit, as well as some more tongue-in-cheek suggestions: the dinkum, the sheepsback and the bobmenz. Treasurer Harold Holt eventually put the controversy to an end by settling on the less distinctive, but least contentious, 'Australian dollar'. Curran and Ward, *The Unknown Nation*, 91–96.

[10] Meaney, 'The United States', pp. 163–166.

[11] Donald Horne, *The Bulletin*, 20 Jan 1968, p. 22.

[12] Policy Planning Paper, 'Developments in Sino-American Relations: Implications for Australia', Canberra, 21 Jul 1971, document 219, in Doran and Lee, *Australia and Recognition of the People's Republic of China, 1949–1972*, pp. 518–525.

[13] In New York, October 1971, as quoted in Robert O'Neill, 'Problems in Australian Foreign Policy, July–December 1971', *The Australian Journal of Politics & History* 18:1 (Apr 1972), pp. 1–17, 2.

[14] 76 in favour, 35 opposed, and 17 abstentions. A.C. Palfreeman, 'Foreign Policy Review', *The Australian Quarterly* 44:2 (Jun 1972), pp. 112–121, 113.

[15] O'Neill, 'Problems in Australian Foreign Policy, July–December 1971', p. 7.

[16] See, for example, Fung, 'Australia's China Policy in Tatters 1971–72'.

[17] Andrews, *Australia and China*, p. 202.

[18] NAA, Bowen, 'China Policy: Information Paper', 17 Feb 1972.

[19] Meaney, *Australia and the World*, document 395, p. 735.

[20] Meaney, 'The United States', pp. 179–180.

[21] Ibid., p. 180.

[22] John Lapsley, 'The U.S. connection', *The Australian*, 13 Aug 1974, p. 10.

[23] U.S. Department of State, Kissinger, 'China Policy', Washington, 19 Nov 1970.

24 Nagano, *A Study of the Foreign Relations*, pp. 4–5; Kissinger, *The White House Years*, p. 762.

25 As recounted in Renouf, *The Frightened Country*, p. 279.

26 NAA, McMahon, 'Australia's policy towards China', 9 Feb 1971, p. 82.

27 Ibid., p. 35.

28 NAA (Sydney), M170, 2002/05249772, 4 'Speeches and interview transcripts for the Hon Edward Gough Whitlam, AC, QC 1971', E.G. Whitlam, Speech given at the ALP Federal Conference, Launceston, 20 Jun 1971.

29 NAA, McMahon, 'Australia's policy towards China', 9 Feb 1971, p. 83.

30 Ibid., p. 82.

31 Holt had turned to Asia with the qualification that Australia would remain 'in essence' a British country. Jeppe Kristensen, '"In Essence still a British Country": Britain's withdrawal from East of Suez', *Australian Journal of Politics and History* 51:1 (2005), pp. 40–52, 52; I.R. Hancock, 'Holt, Harold Edward (1908–1967)', *Australian Dictionary of Biography*, National Centre of Biography, Australian National University, [online] at: http://adb.anu.edu.au/biography/holt-harold-edward-10530/text18693, accessed 2 Sep 2011.

32 Broinowski, *The Yellow Lady*, esp. pp. 198–203.

33 NAA, 'Cabinet Papers on Policy, 1971–1980', McMahon, Cabinet Minute, Sydney, 18 Jul 1971, p. 1.

34 NAA, 'China – Relations with Australia, 1971–72', William McMahon, 'Address to the American-Australian Association Luncheon', Sydney, 17 Apr 1972, p. 5.

35 For example, Whitlam played up the fact that Lyndon Johnson mimicked Labor policy in March 1968 when he began limiting American bombing of North Vietnam. See U.S. Department of State: Office of the Historian, Foreign Relations of the United States, 1964–1968, Volume XXVII, Mainland Southeast Asia, Regional Affairs, Document 36, Telegram

from Secretary of State Rusk to the Department of State, Canberra, 6 Apr 1968.

[36]   As quoted in D.J. Murphy, 'Problems in Australian Foreign Policy, January to June, 1973', *Australian Journal of Politics & History* 19:3 (Dec 1973), pp. 331–342, 331.

[37]   Meaney, *Australia and the World*, document 397, p. 737.

[38]   For archival extracts of the American reaction see Stephen Stockwell, 'Beyond Conspiracy Theory: US presidential archives on the Australian press, national security and the Whitlam government', Refereed paper presented to the Journalism Education Conference, Griffith University, 29 Nov–2 Dec 2005 [online] at: http://www98.griffith.edu.au/dspace/handle/10072/2432, accessed 28 Aug 2011, pp. 6–7.

[39]   U.S. Department of State: Office of the Historian, Foreign Relations of the United States, 1969–1976, Volume E-12, East and Southeast Asia, Document 37, Memcon, Whitlam and Kissinger, Washington, 30 Jul 1973, 10–11 am.

[40]   Alan Bloomfield and Kim Richard Nossal, 'End of an Era? Anti-Americanism in the Australian Labor Party', *Australian Journal of Politics & History* 56:4 (2010), pp. 592–611, 600–601.

[41]   U.S. Department of State: Office of the Historian, Foreign Relations of the United States, 1969–1976, Volume E-12, East and Southeast Asia, Document 30, Memcon, Wilenski and Kissinger, Washington, 2 May 1973, 5:40–6:35 pm.

[42]   Henry S. Albinski, 'Australia and the United States: an Appraisal of the Relationship', *Australian Journal of Politics & History* 29:2 (Aug 1983), pp. 288–300.

[43]   At least this was the word he used to describe it while in Washington. U.S. Department of State: Office of the Historian, Foreign Relations of the United States, 1969–1976, Volume E-12, East and Southeast Asia, Document 39, Memcon, Rogers and Whitlam, Washington, 31 Jul 1973, 2.30 pm.

44 Meaney, 'United States', pp. 180–190; Gregory Pemberton, 'Whitlam and the Labor Tradition', in Lee et al, *Evatt to Evans*, pp. 131–162.

45 A term used by Whitlam. See NAA (Sydney), M170/1, 71/72, 'Personal Papers of Prime Minister E.G. Whitlam', E.G. Whitlam, 'Ministerial statement', 18 Aug 1971, p. 315.

46 Henry S. Albinski, *The Australian-American Security Relationship: A Regional and International Perspective* (St Lucia, QLD: University of Queensland Press, 1982), pp. 223–224.

47 It was an assignment that Whitlam described as 'very flattering' to Australia. U.S. Department of State, Memcon, Rogers and Whitlam, 31 Jul 1973.

48 As Marshall Green acknowledged at the end of his tenure as American Ambassador to Australia, 'Enduring relations cannot be built on the shifting sands of sentiment.' He spent his years in Australia firming up the foundations of the Australia-America relationship. Marshall Green, Speech to the Asia Society of New York, 12 Mar 1975, in Glen St. J. Barclay and Joseph M. Siracusa, *Australian American Relations Since 1945: A Documentary History* (Sydney: Holt, Rinehart and Winston: 1976), pp. 112–114, 113.

49 Kendall, *Within China's Orbit?*, p. 178.

50 See, for example, Strange, *Openings*.

51 See Introduction, esp. nn. 6–8. Biographer Jenny Hocking is right when she says that Australians take many of Whitlam's major policy changes, such as those on China, for granted. See Kate Hannon, 'Whitlam to mark birthday with family', *The Age*, 10 Jul 2009.

52 For the account of the Australian negotiator, see Renouf, *The Frightened Country*, pp. 331–332. The communiqué announcing recognition is reprinted in New Democratic Publications, *China through Australian eyes* (Canterbury, Victoria: New Democratic Publications, 1973), p. 88.

53 As quoted in FitzGerald, *Talking with China*, p. 43.

54 NAA, Whitlam, 'The United States, China and Japan: Australia's Role', 25 Sep 1971.

55 Paraphrasing Evans and Grant, *Australian Foreign Relations*, p. 250.

56 Geoffrey Blainey, 'Our Relations with China: A Backward and Forward Glance', *The Australian Journal of Chinese Affairs* 11, (Jan 1984), pp. 99–104, 99.

57 Stephen FitzGerald, Personal Communication, 16 Aug 2011.

58 Freudenberg, *A Figure of Speech*, p. 124.

59 Minute from Waller to McMahon, 'Foreign Policy Initiatives on China', Canberra, 21 Jul 1971, document 220, in Doran and Lee, *Australia and Recognition of the People's Republic of China, 1949–1972*, p. 526.

60 The number of Australian tourists travelling to China in 1982. Blainey, 'Our Relations with China', p. 100.

61 NAA, 'Various segments – moving images', Whitlam And Chou En Lai Segment, Misc 5154, 1973; Margaret Whitlam, *My Day* (Sydney: William Collins, 1974), pp. 134–139; Allan Barnes, 'Whitlam gets a gay welcome in China', *The Age*, 1 Nov 1973, p. 1. In 2011, on her first Prime Ministerial visit to China, Julia Gillard sought out Whitlam's translator from his 1973 visit, Li Zhong, and arranged a meeting. 'She played a part in what was a historic moment in Australia-China relations', Gillard said. Matthew Franklin, 'Gough Whitlam's Chinese voice found', *The Australian*, 28 Apr 2011.

62 John R. Walker, 'Australian PM in Peking too', *The Montreal Gazette*, 10 Nov 1973, p. 10.

63 Gough Whitlam, 'Speech at the Banquet in Honour of His Excellency Premier Zhou Enlai', Beijing, 3 Nov 1973, in *The Road to China*, pp. 20–21, 20. On return from his China visit, on 6 November 1973, Whitlam formally resigned as Foreign Minister, passing the portfolio over to Donald Willesee. Claire Clark, 'Problems in Australian Foreign Policy, July to December, 1973', *The Australian Journal of Politics and History* 20:1 (1974), 1–10, 2.

64 Goldsworthy et al, 'Reorientation', p. 338.

65 Malcolm Fraser and Margaret Simons, *Malcolm Fraser: The Political Memoirs* (Melbourne: The Miegunyah Press, 2010), esp. pp. 458–463; Strahan, *Australia's China*, pp. 295–296; Colin Mackerras, 'The Australia-China Relationship: A Partnership of Equals?', in Nicholas Thomas, ed., *Re-orienting Australia-China relations: 1972 to the present* (Hants, UK: Ashgate Publishing Limited, 2004), pp. 15–34, 18–19.

66 Garry Woodard, 'Relations Between Australia and the People's Republic of China: An Individual Perspective', *The Australian Journal of Chinese Affairs* 17 (Jan 1987), pp. 143–152, 147.

67 See Strange, *Openings*.

68 Michael Sainsbury, 'Howard rekindles his Chinese connections', *The Australian*, 18 Sep 2010.

69 Kendall, *Within China's Orbit?*, pp. 75–105.

70 China buys more than a quarter of Australia's total exports. Department of Foreign Affairs and Trade, 'Gillard Government Trade Policy Statement: Trading our way to more jobs and prosperity', April 2011 [online] at: http://www.dfat.gov.au/publications/trade/trading-our-way-to-more-jobs-and-prosperity.pdf, accessed 1 May 2011.

71 Evans and Grant, *Australian Foreign Relations*, p. 26.

72 Graham Freudenberg, 'Aspects of Foreign Policy', in Hugh V. Emy, Owen Hughes and Race Mathews, *Whitlam Revisited: Policy Development, Policies and Outcomes* (Sydney: Pluto Press, 1993), pp. 203, 208.

73 Viviani, 'The Whitlam Government's Policy Towards Asia', p. 107.

74 As quoted in O'Neill, 'Problems in Australian Foreign Policy, July–December 1971', p. 6.

75 Alison Broinowski and Anthony Millar, 'Introduction', in Alison Broinowski, *Double Vision* (Canberra: Pandanus Books, 2004), pp. 1–10, 8–9.

Epilogue

[1] This moment is reconstructed from press clippings found in NLA, Francis James Papers, MS 8657, Acc 04/138, Box 2: Francis James, 'I fight China's expulsion order/I cross the border twice', *The Sydney Morning Herald*, 2 Feb 1973, pp. 7–8; Laurie Oakes, 'James goes free today: Spy, say Chinese', *The Sun*, 16 Jan 1973; Anon., 'Peking Makes a Friendly Gesture', *Standard*, 16 Jan 1973; Anon., 'Out of Nowhere', *The New York Times*, 21 Jan 1973; Suzette Meiring, 'Australian "spy" jailed by China goes free today', *South China Morning Post*, 16 Jan 1973; Suzette Meiring, 'Long ordeal ends with faltering steps to freedom', *South China Morning Post*, 17 Jan 1973; Margaret Jones, 'Francis James – a life story of adventure', *The Sydney Morning Herald*, 16 Jan 1973, p. 7; Stephen Nesbit, 'Chinese may free James soon', *The Age*, 23 Dec 1972, p. 1.

[2] Francis James, 'Seven weeks of questions', *The Sydney Morning Herald*, 5 Feb 1973, pp. 7–8; Francis James, 'My secret China trip', *The Sydney Morning Herald*, 9 Feb 1973, p. 7; Francis James, 'I am stripped and searched at the Chinese border', *The Sydney Morning Herald*, 30 Jan 1973, p. 7.

[3] Penrith City Council Library Service, 'Francis James Collection: Imprisonment in China', *Penrith City Council* [online] at: http://www.penrithcity.nsw.gov.au/index.asp?id=2441, accessed 5 Feb 2011; Agnieszka Sobocinska, 'Prisoners of Opinion: Australians in Asian Captivity, 1942–2005', *Australian Studies* 1:1 (2009), pp. 1–28, 11–15.

[4] Laurie Oakes, 'No word in 2 years', *The Sun*, 8 Mar 1972.

[5] Whitlam, *The Whitlam Government*, p. 58.

[6] Whitlam suffered politically for his public silence; in Parliament he was assailed for having abandoned an old friend. Freudenberg, *A Certain Grandeur*, pp. 218–219.

[7] Whitlam, *The Whitlam Government*, p. 58.

[8] Francis James, 'I'm taken to the border – and back', *The Sydney Morning Herald*, 7 Feb 1973, p. 7.

[9] As quoted in Howard, 'Foreign Policy Review', p. 103.

Bibliography

Primary sources (unpublished)

The Association for Diplomatic Studies and Training, Foreign Affairs Oral History Project

Interview with Joseph S. Farland by Charles Stuart Kennedy, 31 Jan 2003, *The Association for Diplomatic Studies and Training, Foreign Affairs Oral History Project* [online] at: http://frontiers.loc.gov/ service/mss/mssmisc/mfdip/2005 %20txt%20files/2004 far02.txt, accessed 5 Aug 2011.

Australian Broadcasting Corporation

Interview with Tom Burns by Geraldine Doogue, 'Whitlam and China', created 8 Jul 2006, *ABC Radio National: Saturday Extra* [online] at: http://www.abc.net.au/radionational/programs/saturdayextra/ whitlam-and-china/3320598, accessed 4 Apr 2011.

Britain Foreign Papers

Britain Foreign Papers (Marlborough, England: Adam Matthew Digital, c2010), FO 371/186997, Political relations: Australia in Great Britain, Foreign Office files for China, 1949–1980. Section III, 1967–1980, A.J. de la Mare reporting on conversation with the leader (G.A. Jockel) of an Australian delegation from the Department of External Affairs to London, 'Australia and the Hard Line', 11 Oct 1966.

Department of Foreign Affairs and Trade

Department of Foreign Affairs and Trade, 'Gillard Government Trade Policy Statement: Trading our way to more jobs and prosperity',

April 2011 [online] at: http://www.dfat.gov.au/publications/trade/
trading-our-way-to-more-jobs-and-prosperity.pdf, accessed 1 May
2011.

National Archives of Australia, Canberra and Sydney

'ALP Delegation 1971 (1)'

NAA (Canberra), A1838, 3107/38/12/7 PART 1, 'ALP Delegation
1971', Inward cablegram to the Department of Foreign Affairs from
Australian Trade Commission in Hong Kong, 2 Jul 1971.

NAA (Canberra), A1838, 3107/38/12/7 PART 1, 'ALP Delegation
1971', Inward cablegram from the Australian Trade Commission in
Hong Kong to the Department of Foreign Affairs, 5 Jul 1971.

NAA (Canberra), A1838, 3107/38/12/7 PART 1, 'ALP Delegation
1971', Letter from J.R. Burgess to R.H. Robertson, Hong Kong, 29
Jun 1971.

NAA (Canberra), A1838, 3107/38/12/7 PART 1, 'ALP Delegation 1971',
Outward cablegram from the Department of External Affairs to the
Australian Embassy in Paris, 10 Jul 1971.

NAA (Canberra), A1838, 3107/38/12/7 PART 1, 'ALP Delegation 1971',
Outward cablegram from the Department of External Affairs to the
Australian Trade Commission in Hong Kong, 23 Jun 1971.

NAA (Canberra), A1838, 3107/38/12/7 PART 1, 'ALP Delegation 1971',
Reuters telegram, 2 Jul 1971.

NAA (Canberra), A1838, 3107/38/12/7 PART 1, 'ALP Delegation 1971',
Reuters telegram, 3 Jul 1971.

NAA (Canberra), A1838, 3107/38/12/7 PART 1, 'ALP Delegation 1971',
Telegram from the Australian Trade Commission to Leslie Bury,
Hong Kong, 5 Jul 1971.

'ALP Delegation 1971 (2)'

NAA (Canberra), A1838, 3107/38/12/7 PART 2, 'ALP Delegation 1971',
David Barnett, 'China Talk with Chou', Peking, 5 Jul 1971.

NAA (Canberra), A1838, 3107/38/12/7 PART 2, 'ALP Delegation 1971',
T.Y. Liu, 'Report on tape of conversation between Chou En-lai, his
interpreter and Mr. G. Whitlam', 7 Sep 1971.

NAA (Canberra), A1838, 3107/38/12/7 PART 2, 'ALP Delegation 1971',
Memcon, Sato and Whitlam, Tokyo, 21 Jul 1971.

'Australia/China Relations – policy'

NAA (Canberra), A4940, C230 'Australia/China Relations – policy',
Percy Spender, 'Relationship between Australia and China', For
Cabinet, Canberra, 19 Feb 1951.

*'Australian trade with communist China, North Vietnam and North
Korea 1958–67'*

NAA (Canberra), A4840 C2284, 'Australian trade with communist
China, North Vietnam and North Korea 1958–67', John Gorton,
'Trade with China', For Cabinet, 16 May 1966.

Australian wheat sales on credit to mainland China

NAA (Canberra), A4940, C2387, 'Australian wheat sales on credit
to mainland China', C.F. Aderman, 'Mainland China – wheat
negotiations', For Cabinet, Canberra, 10 Mar 1966.

'Cabinet Papers on Policy, 1971–1980'

NAA (Canberra), A1838, 3107/38/20 PART 2, 'Cabinet Papers on
Policy, 1971–1980', Cabinet Minute, 'Without Submission –
President Nixon – Visit to China', Canberra, 20 Jul 1971.

NAA (Canberra), A1838, 3107/38/20 PART 2, 'Cabinet Papers on
Policy, 1971–1980', M.J. Wilson, 'China: Briefing Material', 26 Oct
1971, 4(a).

NAA (Canberra), A1838, 3107/38/20 PART 2, 'Cabinet Papers on
Policy, 1971–1980', Nigel Bowen, 'China Policy: Information Paper',
Department of Foreign Affairs, 17 Feb 1972, p. 16.

NAA (Canberra), A1838, 3107/38/20 PART 2, 'Cabinet Papers on

Policy, 1971–1980', William McMahon, 'Australia's policy towards China', Department of External Affairs, 9 Feb 1971, p. 18.

NAA (Canberra), A1838, 3107/38/20 PART 2, 'Cabinet Papers on Policy, 1971–1980', William McMahon, Cabinet Minute, Sydney, 18 Jul 1971, p. 1.

'China – Relations with Australia, 1971–72'

NAA (Canberra), A1838, 3107/38/3 PART 7, 'China – Relations with Australia 1971–72', Dr Graeme Starr (Senior Liberal Research Officer), 'The Australian Government's views on China', 15 Jul 1971.

NAA (Canberra), A1838, 3107/38/3 PART 7, 'China – Relations with Australia, 1971–72', William McMahon to Citizens Club Dinner, Sydney, 13 May 1971.

NAA (Canberra), A1838, 3107/38/3 PART 7, 'China – Relations with Australia, 1971–72', William McMahon, 'Address to the American-Australian Association Luncheon', Sydney, 17 Apr 1972, p. 5.

'China – Review of policy'

NAA (Canberra), A1838, 3107/38/18, 'China – Review of policy', xix, Cablegram to Canberra, 'Top Secret Immediate', Washington, 19 Jul 1971.

'Communist China Trade Policies'

NAA (Canberra), A4940, C2230, 'Communist China Trade Policies', Cabinet Minute, Canberra, 14 Oct 1958.

'Personal Papers of Prime Minister E.G. Whitlam'

NAA (Canberra), M170, 71/31, 'Personal Papers of Prime Minister E.G. Whitlam', E.G. Whitlam, 'President Nixon on China', Statement by the leader of the Opposition, Adelaide, 15 Apr 1971.

NAA (Canberra), M170, 71/85, 'Personal Papers of Prime Minister E.G. Whitlam', E.G. Whitlam, 'The United States, China and Japan:

Australia's Role', Speech to the Institute of International Affairs, Townsville, 25 Sep 1971.

NAA (Sydney), M170, 70/141, Set 1, Box 1, 'Personal Papers of Prime Minister E.G. Whitlam', E.G. Whitlam, 'Australia and China', Article for Community Aid Abroad Journal 'Now', 16 Dec 1970.

NAA (Sydney), M170/1, 71/72, 'Personal Papers of Prime Minister E.G. Whitlam', E.G. Whitlam, 'Ministerial statement', 18 Aug 1971.

NAA (Sydney), M156, 25, 'Personal Papers of Prime Minister E.G. Whitlam', G. Freudenberg (personal), Box 2, newspaper clipping (unspecified), 'Rotary Club guest Press secretary', 13 Jan 1972.

NAA (Sydney), M156, 25, 'Personal Papers of Prime Minister E.G. Whitlam', G. Freudenberg (personal), Box 2, 'Peking Hotel, China', undated.

'Photographic Image'

NAA (Canberra), A1501, A904/1, 'Photographic Image', W. Bundle, 'Australian students about to tour China study a large wall map of Asia', 1957.

NAA (Canberra), A6180, 14/11/73/209, 'Photographic Image', Gough Whitlam's trip to China, 1973.

'Speeches and interview transcripts for the Hon Edward Gough Whitlam, AC, QC 1971'

NAA (Sydney), M170, 2002/05249772, 4 'Speeches and interview transcripts for the Hon Edward Gough Whitlam, AC, QC 1971', E.G. Whitlam, Speech given at the ALP Federal Conference, Launceston, 20 Jun 1971.

'Various segments – moving images'

NAA (Sydney), C475, ARCH 99F/0368, 'Various segments – moving images', 2–7 Jul 1971, program NPZ628/VISP1925.

NAA (Sydney), C475, ARCH 99F/0368, 'Various segments – moving images', Whitlam in China with Chou, program NPZ634.

NAA (Sydney), C475, ARCH 99F/0368, 'Various segments – moving images', 2–7 Jul 1971, program NPZ639.

NAA (Sydney), C475, ARCH 99F/0368, 'Various segments – moving images', 2–7 Jul 1971, program NPZ641.

NAA (Sydney), C475, ARCH 09F/1596, 'Various segments – moving images', Whitlam And Chou En Lai Segment, Misc 5154, 1973.

National Library of Australia, Canberra

Anon., 'Gough Whitlam speaking to unidentified journalists upon returning from his visit to China', 1971, *Digital Collections* [online] at: http://nla.gov.au/nla.pic-an24507693, accessed 28 Sep 2011.

Eggleston, Frederic, *Diaries 1941–1946*, [microform] Series 9, Items 376–1425 at NLA, Bib ID 2090183, mfm G 24016–24018, Prose Diary.

Fitzgerald, Stephen, An ANU Convocation luncheon address given on the subject of China, 1 Dec 1976, [sound recording] at NLA, Bib ID 428102.

Clyde Cameron Papers

Mick Young telegram to Clyde Cameron 12 May 1971, at NLA, Clyde Cameron Papers, MS4614, Box 5, Folder 1.

Richard Hall Papers

E.M. Manac'h telegram to Ross Terrill, 10 May 1971, at NLA, Richard Hall Papers, MS8725, Box 51, Series 15, Folder 2.

Outward Cablegram from Gough Whitlam to Premier Zhou Enlai, Peking, China, 14 Apr 1971, in NLA, Richard Hall Papers, MS8725, Series 15, Box 51, Folder 2.

Ross Terrill letter to E.M. Manac'h, 28 Apr 1971, at NLA, Richard Hall Papers, MS8725, Box 51, Series 15, Folder 2.

Ross Terrill, New York Times Commission, Draft to Richard Hall, undated, at NLA, Richard Hall Papers, MS8725, Box 51, Series 15, Folder 2.

Ross Terrill letter to Richard Hall, undated (c. 28 Apr 1971), at NLA,

Richard Hall Papers, MS8725, Box 51, Series 15, Folder 2.

Ross Terrill letter to Richard Hall, 28 Apr 1971, at NLA, Richard Hall Papers, MS8725, Box 51, Series 15, Folder 2.

Parliamentary Documents

Chifley, Ben, 'International Affairs', House of Representatives, *Debates*, 7 Mar 1951, p. 85.

Evatt, H.V., *Current Notes on International Affairs* 20 (Oct 1949), pp. 1084–1085.

Evatt, H.V., 'International Affairs', House of Representatives, *Debates*, 16 Mar 1950, p. 919.

Leslie, Hugh, 'International Affairs', House of Representatives, *Debates*, 12 Aug 1954, pp. 276–278.

Menzies, R.G., 'International Affairs', House of Representatives, *Debates*, 5 Aug 1954, pp. 65–66.

Menzies, R.G., 'Vietnam–Ministerial Statement', House of Representatives, Debates, 29 Apr 1965, pp.1060–1.

Spender, Percy, 'International Affairs', House of Representatives, *Debates*, 9 Mar 1950, p. 621–41.

Whitlam, Gough, 'International Affairs', House of Representatives, *Debates*, 12 Aug 1954, pp. 272–276.

The Whitlam Institute, Sydney

E.G. Whitlam, 'Australia – Base or Bridge?', 16 Sep 1966, University of Sydney, *Whitlam Institute e-collection*.

E.G. Whitlam, 'Australian Foreign Policy 1963', 9 Jul 1963, The Australian Institute of International Affairs, Whitlam Institute e-collection.

E.G. Whitlam, 'Leader of the Opposition: Chinese Delegation', 13 Sep 1977, Canberra, *Whitlam Institute e-collection*.

E.G. Whitlam, Press Release, 'Proposed Visit to China – 1971', 11 May 1971, *Whitlam Institute e-collection*.

E.G. Whitlam, 'What Should Australia's Foreign Policy Be?', 23 Jan 1961, University of Western Australia, *Whitlam Institute e-collection*.

Personal Communication

Stephen FitzGerald, Personal Communication, 16 Aug 2011.

U.S. Department of State: Office of the Historian

Foreign Relations of the United States, 1964–1968

U.S. Department of State: Office of the Historian, Foreign Relations of the United States, 1964–1968, Volume XXVII, Mainland Southeast Asia, Regional Affairs, Document 36, Telegram from Secretary of State Rusk to the Department of State, Canberra, 6 Apr 1968.

Foreign Relations of the United States, 1967–1976

U.S. Department of State: Office of the Historian, Foreign Relations of the United States, 1967–1976, Volume XVII, China, 1969–1972, Document 97, National Security Study Memorandum 106, Henry A. Kissinger, 'China Policy', Washington, 19 Nov 1970.

Foreign Relations of the United States, 1969–1976

U.S. Department of State: Office of the Historian, Foreign Relations of the United States, 1969–1976, Volume E-12, East and Southeast Asia, Document 30, Memcon, Wilenski and Kissinger, Washington, 2 May 1973, 5:40–6:35 pm.

U.S. Department of State: Office of the Historian, Foreign Relations of the United States, 1969–1976, Volume E-12, East and Southeast Asia, Document 37, Memcon, Whitlam and Kissinger, Washington, 30 Jul 1973, 10–11 am.

U.S. Department of State: Office of the Historian, Foreign Relations of the United States, 1969–1976, Volume E-12, East and Southeast Asia, Document 39, Memcon, Rogers and Whitlam, Washington, 31 Jul 1973, 2.30 pm.

Primary sources (published)

Burr, William, ed., 'National Security Archive Electronic Briefing Book
No. 66: September 1970 – July 1971', *The National Security Archive*,
27 Feb 2002 [online] at: http://www.gwu. edu/~nsarchiv/NS AEBB/
NSAEBB66/#docs, accessed 4 Aug 2011.

>Henry Kissinger to Richard Nixon, 'My Talks with Zhou Enlai,' 14
Jul 1971, document 40.

>Memcon, Henry Kissinger and Zhou Enlai, 9 Jul 1971, 4:35–11:20
pm, document 34.

>Memcon, Henry Kissinger and Zhou Enlai, 11 Jul 1971, 10:35–
11:55 am, document 38.

>Memcon, Henry Kissinger and Ye Jianying, 11 Jul 1971, 12 – 1.40
am, 9.50 – 10.35 am, document 37.

>Memorandum for the President's Files, 'Briefing of the White
House Staff on the July 15', 19 Jul 1971, document 41.

Clark, Gregory, *Life Story*, 2005 [online] at: http://www.gregoryclark.net/,
accessed 24 Jun 2011.

Doran, Stuart (and David Lee), eds, *Documents on Australian Foreign
Policy: Australia and Recognition of the People's Republic of China,
1949–1972* (Canberra: Department for Foreign Affairs, 2002).

>Brief for Australian Delegation to the Geneva Conference, Canberra,
undated, document 45, pp. 79–82.

>Cablegram to New York, For Spender only from Menzies, Canberra,
21 Oct 1950, document 21, pp. 28–29.

>Cablegram to Paris, For Renouf, Canberra, 1 Jul 1971, document
201, pp. 483–484.

>Cablegram to Canberra, Emergency, For Prime Minister from
Plimsoll, Washington, 15 Jul 1971, document 209, p. 502.

>Cablegram to Canberra, Paris, 2 Jul 1971, document 202, pp. 485–
486.

>Cablegram to Washington, For Nixon c/o Plimsoll from McMahon,
Canberra, 18 Jul 1971, document 213, pp. 509–510.

Minute from Waller to McMahon, 'Foreign Policy Initiatives on China', Canberra, 21 Jul 1971, document 220, p. 526.

Policy Planning Paper, 'Developments in Sino-American Relations: Implications for Australia', Canberra, 21 Jul 1971, document 219, pp. 518–525.

FitzGerald, Stephen, 'The Bogey-Man Vanishes', *The Far Eastern Economic Review*, 11 Sep 1971, pp. 32–34.

FitzGerald, Stephen, *China and the World* (Canberra: Contemporary China Centre in association with Australian University Press, 1977).

FitzGerald, Stephen, 'China in the Next Decade: An End to Isolation?', *Australian Journal of Politics & History* 17:1 (Apr 1971), pp. 33–43.

FitzGerald, Stephen, 'Impressions of China's New Diplomacy: The Australian Experience', *The China Quarterly* 48 (Oct–Dec 1971), pp. 670–676.

FitzGerald, Stephen, *Talking with China: The Australian Labor Party visit and Peking's foreign policy* (Canberra: Australian National University Press, 1972).

Fraser, Malcolm (and Margaret Simons), *Malcolm Fraser: The Political Memoirs* (Melbourne: The Miegunyah Press, 2010).

Freudenberg, Graham, *A Certain Grandeur* (Camberwell, Victoria: Viking, 2009).

Freudenberg, Graham, *A Figure of Speech: A Political Memoir* (Milton, QLD: Wiley, 2005).

Green, Marshall, Speech to the Asia Society of New York, 12 Mar 1975, in Glen St. J. Barclay and Joseph M. Siracusa, *Australian American Relations Since 1945: A Documentary History* (Sydney: Holt, Rinehart and Winston: 1976), pp. 112–114.

Green, Marshall, 'Omens of Change', in Marshall Green et al, *War and Peace with China: First hand experiences in the foreign service of the United States* (Maryland: DACOR Press, 1994).

Holdridge, John H., 'Through China's back door' in Marshall Green et al, *War and Peace with China: First hand experiences in the foreign service of the United States* (Maryland: DACOR Press, 1994).

Howson, Peter (ed. Don Aitkin), *The Howson Diaries: The Life of Politics* (Ringwood, VIC: The Viking Press, 1984).

Kissinger, Henry, *The White House Years* (Sydney: Hodder and Stoughton, 1979).

Manac'h, Etienne M., *La Chine* (Paris: Librairie Arthème Fayard, 1980).

Nixon, Richard M., 'Asia after Viet Nam', *Foreign Affairs* 46 (1967–68), pp. 111–125.

Oakes, Laurie, *Whitlam P.M.* (Sydney: Angus and Robertson, 1973).

Oakes, Laurie (and David Solomon), *The Making of An Australian Prime Minister* (St. Kilda, Melbourne: Cheshire Publishing Pty Ltd, 1973).

Renouf, Alan, *The Frightened Country* (Melbourne: MacMillan Company, 1979).

Terrill, Ross, *800,000,000: The Real China* (London: Heinemann, 1972).

Terrill, Ross, 'Australia and China', *Nation*, 7 Aug 1971, pp. 12–14.

Waller, Keith, *A Diplomatic Life: Some Memories*, Australians in Asia Series No. 6 (Nathan, Queensland: Griffith University Press, 1990).

Whitlam, Gough, 'Foreword', in Georg Gerster et al, *Over China* (North Ryde, NSW: Angus & Robertson Publishers, 1988), pp. 15–16.

Whitlam, Gough, *The Road to China* (Hong Kong: Cosmos Books, 2010).

'A Memorable Night 31 Years Ago', Shanghai, 2 Aug 2002, pp. 57–65.

'Human Rights: Problem of Selective Memories', Sydney, 11 Dec 1997, pp. 179–194.

'Speech at the Banquet in Honour of His Excellency Premier Zhou Enlai', Beijing, 3 Nov 1973, pp. 20–21.

'The Great Wall of China', Sydney, 27 Sep 2006, pp. 22–28.

'The Proper Course for Business with China Benefits All', Beijing, 29 Jul 2002, pp. 100–109.

'The Real Value of My First Visit to China', Crown Casino Palladium, 9 Dec 2002, pp. 7–13.

Whitlam, Gough, *The Whitlam Government 1972–1975* (Ringwood, Victoria: Viking, 1985).

Whitlam, Margaret, *My Day* (Sydney: William Collins, 1974).

Newspaper sources

Anon., 'Australian Table Tennis Delegation Visits China', *Peking Review*, 7 May 1971, p. 30.

Anon., 'Dialogue in Peking', *The Age*, 7 Jul 1971, p. 9.

Anon., 'Dismay in Taiwan: Tokyo Welcomes Plan', *The New York Times*, 17 Jul 1971, p. 1.

Anon., 'Dr Patterson sounds out China export hopes', *Canberra News*, 7 Jul 1971.

Anon., 'Ducking Off to Peking', *The Canberra Times*, 17 Jun 1971.

Anon., 'The Inscrutable Occidental: Henry Alfred Kissinger', *The New York Times*, 17 Jul 1971, p. 2.

Anon., 'P.M. says: it's also our policy', *The Sydney Morning Herald*, 17 Jul 1971, p. 1.

Anon., 'Labor's China visitors ready', *The Sydney Morning Herald*, 4 Jul 1971, p. 2.

Anon., 'Labor's Five Leave for China Visit', *The Australian*, 28 Jun 1971.

Anon., 'Labor team off to China', *The Age*, 28 Jun 1971.

Anon., 'Nixon Breakthrough', *The Australian*, 17 Jul 1971, p. 1.

Anon., 'No Common Sense by Peking, Says PM', *The Sydney Morning Herald*, 5 Jul 1971, p. 1.

Anon., 'Out of Nowhere', *The New York Times*, 21 Jan 1973.

Anon., 'Peking Makes a Friendly Gesture', *Standard*, 16 Jan 1973.

Anon., 'President R. Nixon Plans Visit', *Asian Recorder*, 6 – 12 Aug 1971, pp. 10292–10293.

Anon., 'Press agony over China', *The Review*, 4 Jul 1971.

Anon., 'Restoration of International Ties', *Asian Recorder*, 16 – 22 Jul 1971, pp. 10258–10259.

Anon., 'Santamaria: Whitlam Chinese candidate', *The Sydney Morning Herald*, 12 Jul 1971, p. 2.

Anon., 'Taiwan Lodges a Protest', *The New York Times*, 16 Jul 1971, p. 1.

Anon., 'Trudeau Commends Nixon's "Bold" Step', *The New York Times*, 17 Jul 1971, p. 2.

Anon., 'Well done, Mr. Pepin', *The Montreal Gazette*, 6 Jul 1971, p. 6.

Anon., 'Whitlam Used By Chou—PM', *The Age*, 13 Jul 1971, p. 1.

Barnes, Allan, 'Battle of wits in Great Hall of the People', *The Age*, 7 Jul 1971, p. 1.

Barnes, Allan, 'Centre-stage with the maestro', *The Age*, 12 Jan 1976, p. 7.

Barnes, Allan, 'Whitlam gets a gay welcome in China', *The Age*, 1 Nov 1973, p. 1.

Bennett, John, 'Selling goods to China', *The Age*, 12 Apr 1966.

Franklin, Matthew, 'Gough Whitlam's Chinese voice found', *The Australian*, 28 Apr 2011.

Grant, Bruce, 'Whitlam did himself proud', *The Age*, 8 Jul 1971.

Hannon, Kate, 'Whitlam Joint Legacy Honoured', *The Canberra Times*, 29 Apr 2007.

Hannon, Kate, 'Whitlam to mark birthday with family', *The Age*, 10 Jul 2009.

Hart, Jeffrey, 'Conservatives Riled By Nixon China Policy', *The Evening Independent*, 28 Jul 1971, p. 12.

Horne, Donald, *The Bulletin*, 20 Jan 1968.

James, Francis, 'I am stripped and searched at the Chinese border', *The Sydney Morning Herald*, 30 Jan 1973, p. 7.

James, Francis, 'I'm taken to the border—and back', *The Sydney Morning Herald*, 7 Feb 1973, p. 7.

James, Francis, 'I fight China's expulsion order/I cross the border twice', *The Sydney Morning Herald*, 2 Feb 1973, pp. 7–8.

James, Francis, 'My secret China trip', *The Sydney Morning Herald*, 9 Feb 1973, p. 7.

James, Francis, 'Seven weeks of questions', *The Sydney Morning Herald*, 5 Feb 1973, pp. 7–8.

Jones, Margaret, 'Francis James—a life story of adventure', *The Sydney Morning Herald*, 16 Jan 1973, p. 7.

Lapsley, John, 'The U.S. connection', *The Australian*, 13 Aug 1974, p. 10.

Marr, David, 'We need to talk about Kevin ... Rudd that is', *The Sydney Morning Herald*, 7 Jun 2010.

Meiring, Suzette, 'Australian "spy" jailed by China goes free today', *South China Morning Post*, 16 Jan 1973.

Meiring, Suzette, 'Long ordeal ends with faltering steps to freedom', *South*

China Morning Post, 17 Jan 1973.

Nesbit, Stephen, 'Chinese may free James soon', *The Age*, 23 Dec 1972, p. 1.

Oakes, Laurie, 'James goes free today: Spy, say Chinese', *The Sun*, 16 Jan 1973.

Oakes, Laurie, 'No word in 2 years', *The Sun*, 8 Mar 1972.

O Farrell, John, 'Chou had Whitlam on a hook, says PM', *The Sydney Morning Herald*, 13 Jul 1971, p. 1.

Randall, Kenneth, 'Cable from Peking Embarrasses McMahon: Whitlam Going to China', *The Australian*, 12 May 1971.

Randall, Kenneth, 'A hug and an apology in Peking', *The Australian*, 9 Jul 1971.

Randall, Kenneth, 'Open Door to Peking', *The Australian*, 2 Jul 1971.

Sainsbury, Michael, 'Howard rekindles his Chinese connections', *The Australian*, 18 Sep 2010.

Solomon, David, 'ALP Boat to China hits Stormy Seas', *The Canberra Times*, 25 May 1971.

Starr, Frank, 'Praise Nixon's China Visit', *Chicago Tribune*, 17 Jul 1971, p. 1.

Stubbs, John, 'A memorable birthday', *The Sydney Morning Herald*, 13 Jul 1971, p. 7.

Stubbs, John, 'Recognition Bid', *The Sydney Morning Herald*, 5 Jul 1971, p. 1.

Stubbs, John, 'Whitlam and Chou argue on US pact', *The Sydney Morning Herald*, 7 Jul 1971, p. 1.

Sweeris, Connie (as told to Tony Dokoupil), 'From Ping-Pong To Pyongyang', *Newsweek*, 10 Mar 2008.

Terrill, Ross 'Nixon Visit Has Chinese Both Curious and Confused', *The Tuscaloosa News*, 23 Jul 1971, p. 14.

Walker, John R., 'China to buy more wheat', *The Montreal Gazette*, 7 Jul 1971, p. 21.

Walker, John R. 'Australian PM in Peking too', *The Montreal Gazette*, 10 Nov 1973, p. 10.

Warden, Philip, 'Called Astute Political Move: Congress Hails Nixon's Plans to Visit China', The *Chicago Tribune*, 17 Jul 1971, p. 1.

Whitlam, Gough, 'China and the U.S.', *The Australian*, 18 Jul 1971, p. 15.

Whitlam, Gough, 'Dateline: Peking', *The Australian*, 11 Jul 1971, p.11.

Whitlam, Gough, 'My Mission to China', *The Australian*, 4 Jul 1971, p. 2.

Xinhua, 'Lo Wu Bridge on HK-Shenzhen borders witnesses China's reform and opening-up', *People's Daily*, 6 Sep 2010, p. 4.

Secondary sources

Albinski, Henry S., 'Australia and the China Problem Under the Labor Government', *Australian Journal of Politics & History* 10:2 (Aug 1964), pp. 149–172.

Albinski, Henry S., 'Australia and the United States: an Appraisal of the Relationship', *Australian Journal of Politics & History* 29:2 (Aug 1983), pp. 288–300.

Albinski, Henry S., Australian *External Policy Under Labour* (University of Queensland Press, Brisbane, 1977).

Albinski, Henry S., *Australian Policies and Attitudes Toward China* (Princeton, New Jersey: Princeton University Press, 1965).

Albinski, Henry S., *The Australian-American Security Relationship: A Regional and International Perspective* (St Lucia, QLD: University of Queensland Press, 1982).

Andrews, E.M., 'Australia and China, 1949: The Failure to Recognise the PRC', *The Australian Journal of Chinese Affairs* 13 (Jan 1985), pp. 29–50.

Andrews, E.M., *Australia and China: The Ambiguous Relationship* (Melbourne: Melbourne University Press, 1985).

Anon., 'Quarterly Chronicle and Documentation', *The China Quarterly* 48 (Oct–Dec 1971), pp. 783–817.

Anon., 'Timeline', *Free China Review* 21:8 (Aug 1971), pp. 45–48.

Atkinson, Joel, 'Australian Support for an Independent Taiwan Prior to the Recognition of the People's Republic of China', *Australian Journal of Politics & History* 57:1 (2011), pp. 68–85.

Barrett, Lindsay, *The Prime Minister's Christmas Card: Blue Poles and cultural politics in the Whitlam era* (Sydney: Power Publications, 2001).

Beckwith, Christopher I., *Empires of the Silk Road: A History of Central Eurasia from the Bronze Age to the Present* (Princeton: Princeton University Press, 2009).

Bell, Roger, 'The American Influence', in Neville Meaney, ed., *Under New Heavens: Cultural Transmission and the Making of Australia* (Sydney: Heinemann Educational Australia, 1989), pp. 325–377.

Bernstein, Carl (and Bob Woodward), *All the president's men* (New York: Simon and Schuster, 1974).

Bettmann, 'Richard Nixon Conversing with William McMahon', *Corbis Images* (2011) [online] at: http://www.corbisimages.com/stock-photo/rights-managed/SF37825/ richard-nixon-conversing-with-william-mcmahon?popup=1, accessed 28 Sep 2011.

Blanchette, Arthur E., *Canadian foreign policy, 1945–2000: major documents and speeches* (Kemptville, Canada: The Golden Dog Press, 2000).

Blainey, Geoffrey, 'Our Relations with China: A Backward and Forward Glance', *The Australian Journal of Chinese Affairs* 11, (Jan, 1984), pp. 99–104.

Bloomfield, Alan (and Kim Richard Nossal), 'End of an Era? Anti-Americanism in the Australian Labor Party', *Australian Journal of Politics & History* 56:4 (2010), pp. 592–611.

Broinowski, Alison (and Anthony Millar), 'Introduction', in Alison Broinowski, *Double Vision* (Canberra: Pandanus Books, 2004), pp. 1–10.

Broinowski, Alison, *The Yellow Lady: Australian Impressions of Asia* (Melbourne: Oxford University Press, 1992).

Burton, John, *The alternative: a dynamic approach to our relations with Asia* (Sydney: Morgans Publications, 1954).

Camilleri, Joseph, 'Foreign Policy', in Allan Patience and Brian Head, eds, *From Whitlam to Fraser: Reform and Reaction in Australian Politics* (Melbourne: Oxford University Press, 1979).

Carroll, Brian, *Whitlam* (Kenthurst, NSW: Rosenberg Publishing Pty Ltd, 2011).

Clark, Claire, 'Problems in Australian Foreign Policy, July to December, 1973', *The Australian Journal of Politics and History* 20:1 (1974), 1–10.

Clark, Gregory, *In Fear of China* (Melbourne: Lansdowne, 1967).

Collingwood, R.G., *An Autobiography* (London: Oxford University Press, 1939).

Curran, James, *The Power of Speech: Australian Prime Ministers Defining the National Image* (Melbourne: Melbourne University Press, 2004).

Curran, James (and Stuart Ward), *The Unknown Nation* (Melbourne: Melbourne University Press, 2010).

Evans, Gareth (and Bruce Grant), *Australian Foreign Relations: In the World of the 1990s* (Melbourne: Melbourne University Press, second edition 1995).

Fitzgerald, C.P., 'China, Korea and Indo-China', in Gordon Greenwood, ed., *Australian Policies Toward Asia: Part VI* (Melbourne: Australian Institute of International Affairs, 1954).

Farnsworth, Malcolm, 'It's Time', *whitlamdismissal.com* (2010) [online] at: http://whitlamdismissal.com/whitlam/its-time.shtml, accessed 12 Sep 2011.

Freudenberg, Graham, 'Aspects of Foreign Policy', in Hugh V. Emy, Owen Hughes and Race Mathews, *Whitlam Revisited: Policy Development, Policies and Outcomes* (Sydney: Pluto Press, 1993).

Fung, Edmund S.K., 'Australia's China Policy in Tatters 1971–72', *The Australian Journal of Chinese Affairs* 10 (Jul 1983), pp. 39–59.

Fung, Edmund S.K. (and Colin Mackerras), *From Fear to Friendship: Australia's Policies towards the People's Republic of China* (St Lucia, QLD: University of Queensland Press, 1985).

Golding, Peter, *Black Jack McEwen: Political Gladiator* (Melbourne: Melbourne University Press, 1996).

Goldsworthy, David, et al, 'Reorientation', in David Goldsworthy, ed., *Facing North: A Century of Australian Engagement with Asia, Volume 1: 1901 to the 1970s* (Melbourne: Melbourne University Press, 2001), pp. 310–371.

Granatstein, J.L. (and Robert Bothwell), *Pirouette: Pierre Trudeau and Canadian Foreign Policy* (Toronto: University of Toronto Press, 1990).

H, C.A., 'Australian Political Chronicle May-August 1971', *The Australian Journal of Politics & History* 17:3 (Dec 1971), pp. 416–428.

Hancock, I.R., 'Holt, Harold Edward (1908–1967)', *Australian Dictionary of Biography*, National Centre of Biography, Australian National University, [online] at: http://adb.anu.edu.au/biography/holt-harold-edward-10530/text 18693, accessed 2 Sep 2011.

Hayden, Bill, 'Australia's China Policy Under Labor', *The Australian Journal of Chinese Affairs* 11 (Jan 1984), pp. 83–97.

Hayden, Bill, *Hayden: An Autobiography* (Sydney: Angus & Robertson, 1996).

Hocking, Jenny, *Gough Whitlam: A Moment in History* (Melbourne: Melbourne University Press, 2008).

Hocking, Jenny, 'Post-War Reconstruction and the New World Order: The Origins of Gough Whitlam's Democratic Citizen', *Australian Journal of Politics & History* 53:2 (2007), pp. 223–235.

Howard, Bob, 'Foreign Policy Review', *The Australian Quarterly* 43:3 (Sep 1971), pp. 97–108.

Johnson, Carol, et al, 'Australia's Ambivalent Re-imagining of Asia', *Australian Journal of Political Science*, 45:1 (Feb 2010), pp. 59–74.

Keith, Ronald C., *The Diplomacy of Zhou Enlai* (London: The MacMillan Press, 1989).

Kendall, Timothy, *Within China's Orbit? China through the Eyes of the Australian Parliament* (Canberra: Department of Parliamentary Services, Parliament of Australia, 2008).

Kent, Ann, 'Australia-China Relations, 1966–1996: A Critical Overview', *Australian Journal of Politics and History* 42:3 (Aug 1996), pp. 365–84.

Kertzer, David I., *Ritual, Politics, and Power* (New Haven: Yale University Press, 1988).

Khanna, Parag, *The Second World: How Emerging Powers are Redefining Global Competition in the Twenty-first Century* (London: Penguin Books, 2008).

Klintworth, Gary, *Australia's Taiwan Policy 1942–1992*, (Canberra: Australian Foreign Policy Papers, The Australian National University, 1993).

Kristensen, Jeppe, '"In Essence still a British Country": Britain's withdrawal from East of Suez', *Australian Journal of Politics and History* 51:1 (2005), pp. 40–52.

Leeser, Julian, 'Sir William McMahon (1908–1988)', *Australian Dictionary of Biography*, forthcoming.

Mackerras, Colin, 'The Australia-China Relationship: A Partnership of Equals?', in Nicholas Thomas, ed., *Re-orienting Australia-China relations: 1972 to the present* (Hants, UK: Ashgate Publishing Limited, 2004), pp. 15–34.

MacMillan, Margaret, *Nixon and Mao: the week that changed the world* (New York: Random House, 2007).

Mah, Feng-hwa, 'Comment: Why China Imports Wheat', *The China Quarterly* 48 (Oct–Dec 1971), pp. 738–740.

Maloney, Shane (and Chris Grosz), *Australian Encounters* (Melbourne: Black Inc., 2010).

Megalogenis, George, *The Australian Moment: How we were made for these times* (Camberwell, Victoria: Viking, 2012).

Murphy, D.J., 'Problems in Australian Foreign Policy, January to June, 1973', *Australian Journal of Politics & History* 19:3 (Dec 1973), pp. 331–342.

Murray, Robert, *The Split: Australian Labor in the Fifties* (Melbourne: Cheshire, 1970).

Myers, Ramon H., 'Wheat in China—Past, Present and Future', *The China Quarterly* 74 (Jun 1978), pp. 297–333.

Meaney, Neville, 'Australia and the World', in Neville Meaney, ed., *Under New Heavens: Cultural Transmission and the Making of Australia* (Sydney: Heinemann Educational Australia, 1989), pp. 379–450.

Meaney, Neville, ed., *Australia and the world: a documentary history from the 1870s to the 1970s*, (Melbourne: Longman Cheshire, 1985).

Meaney, Neville, 'Frederic Eggleston on International Relations and Australia's Role in the World', *Australian Journal of Politics & History* 51:3 (2005), pp. 359–371.

Meaney, Neville, 'The United States' in W.J. Hudson, ed., *Australia in World Affairs*, 1971–75 (Sydney: George Allen & Unwin, 1980), pp. 163–208.

Miyagawa, Osamu, *The impact of the Nixon shock on Japanese foreign policy toward China and Japanese economic policy* (Texas: Texas Tech University, 1987).

Millar, T.B., *Australia in Peace and War: External Relations 1788–1977* (Canberra, Australian National University Press, 1978).

Nagano, Nobutoshi, *A Study of the Foreign Relations* (Tokyo: Simul Press, 1975).

National Archives of Australia, 'Timeline: Gough Whitlam', *Australia's Prime Ministers* [online] at: http://primeministers.naa.gov.au/ timeline/results.aspx ?type=pm&pm= Gough%20Whitlam, accessed 2 Sep 2011.

New Democratic Publications, *China through Australian eyes* (Canterbury, Victoria: New Democratic Publications, 1973).

Oakes, Laurie, et al, *Whitlam and Frost* (Kent Town, SA: Sundial Publications, 1974).

O'Neill, Robert, 'Problems in Australian Foreign Policy, July–December 1971', *The Australian Journal of Politics & History* 18:1 (Apr 1972), pp. 1–17.

Osmond, Warren G., *Frederic Eggleston: An intellectual in Australian Politics* (Sydney: Allen & Unwin, 1985).

Palfreeman, A.C., 'Foreign Policy Review', *The Australian Quarterly* 44:2 (Jun 1972), pp. 112–121.

Pemberton, Gregory, 'Whitlam and the Labor Tradition', in David Lee and Christopher Waters, *Evatt to Evans: The Labor Tradition in Australian Foreign Policy* (Sydney: Allen & Unwin, 1997), pp. 131–162.

Penrith City Council Library Service, 'Francis James Collection: Imprisonment in China', *Penrith City Council* [online] at: http://www. penrithcity.nsw.gov.au /index.asp?id =2441, accessed 5 Feb 2011.

Perkins, Dwight H., 'China's economic policy and performance', in Denis Crispin Twitchett and John King Fairbank, eds, *The Cambridge history of China, Volume 1* (Melbourne: University of Cambridge Press, 1991), pp. 475–539.

Phillips, P.D., 'War Trends in Australian Opinions' in *Australian Institute of International Affairs, Australia and the Pacific* (Princeton: Princeton University Press, 1944).

Pitty, Roderic, 'Way behind in following the USA over China: The Lack of any Liberal Tradition in Australian Foreign Policy, 1970–72', *Australian Journal of Politics & History* 51:3 (2005), pp. 440–450.

Pollack, Jonothan D., 'The Opening to America', in Denis Crispin Twitchett and John King Fairbank, eds, *The Cambridge history of China, Volume 1* (Melbourne: University of Cambridge Press, 1991), pp. 402–474.

Reynolds, P.L. *The Democratic Labor Party* (Melbourne: The Jacaranda Press, 1974).

Reynolds, Wayne, 'Labor Tradition, Global Shifts and the Foreign Policy of the Whitlam Government', in David Lee and Christopher Waters, *Evatt to Evans: The Labor Tradition in Australian Foreign Policy* (Sydney: Allen & Unwin, 1997), pp. 110–130.

Rolls, Eric, *Sojourners: The epic story of China's centuries-old relationship with Australia* (St Lucia, QLD: University of Queensland Press, 1992).

Ross, Robert S., *Negotiating cooperation: the United States and China, 1969–1989* (Stanford: Stanford University Press, 1995), pp. 17–54.

Rudd, Kevin, 'Foreword: The Road to China', in Gough Whitlam, *The Road to China* (Hong Kong: Cosmos Books, 2010), pp. 5–6.

Sawyer, Diane, 'U.S. and China Through the Years', *ABC World News* (2011) [online] at: http://abcnews.go.com/WN/China/fullpage?id=5444365, accessed 12 Sep 2011.

Sekuless, Peter, 'Sir William McMahon', in Michelle Grattan, ed., *Australian Prime Ministers* (Chatswood, NSW: New Holland Publishers, 2010), pp. 312–323.

Smith, R.F.L., 'Political Review', *The Australian Quarterly* 43:2 (Jun 1971), pp. 110–120.

Sobocinska, Agnieszka, 'Prisoners of Opinion: Australians in Asian Captivity, 1942–2005', *Australian Studies* 1:1 (2009), pp. 1–28.

Stockwell, Stephen, 'Beyond Conspiracy Theory: US presidential archives on the Australian press, national security and the Whitlam government', Refereed paper presented to the Journalism Education Conference, Griffith University, 29 Nov–2 Dec 2005 [online] at: http://www98.griffith.edu.au/dspace/handle/10072 /2432, accessed 28 Aug 2011.

Strahan, Lachlan, *Australia's China: Changing Perceptions from the 1930s to the 1990s* (Melbourne: University of Cambridge Press, 1996).

Strange, Larry, ed., *Openings: A Celebration of the 30th Anniversary of Diplomatic Relations Between Australia and China* (Sydney: The Community Relations Commission For a Multicultural NSW, 2002).

Thomson, Jr., James C., 'On the Making of U. S. China Policy, 1961–9: A Study in Bureaucratic Politics', *The China Quarterly* 50 (Apr–Jun 1972), pp. 220–243.

Viviani, Nancy, 'The Whitlam Government's Policy Towards Asia' in David Lee and Christopher Waters, *Evatt to Evans: The Labor Tradition in Australian Foreign Policy* (Sydney: Allen & Unwin, 1997), pp. 99–109.

Waldron, Arthur, 'Friendship Reconsidered', *Taiwan Review*, 4 Jan 1993 [online] at: http://taiwanreview.nat.gov.tw/ct.asp?xItem=99296&CtNode=1347, accessed 6 Jun 2011.

Walker, David, *Anxious Nation: Australia and the Rise of Asia 1850–1939* (St Lucia, QLD: University of Queensland Press, 1999).

Walker, David (and John Ingleson), 'The Impact of Asia' in Neville Meaney, ed., *Under New Heavens: Cultural Transmission and the Making of Australia* (Sydney: Heinemann Educational Australia, 1989), pp. 287–324.

Walter, James, *The Leader: A Political Biography of Gough Whitlam* (St Lucia, QLD: University of Queensland Press, 1980).

Ward, Stuart, *Australia and the British Embrace: The Demise of the Imperial Ideal* (Melbourne: Melbourne University Press, 2001).

Watt, Alan, *The Evolution of Australian Foreign Policy 1938–1965* (London: Cambridge University Press, 1967).

White, Richard, 'Australian journalists, travel writing and China: James Hingston, the "Vagabond" and G.E. Morrison', *Journal of Australian Studies* 32:2 (2008), pp. 237–250.

Wilson, I.F.H., 'China' in W.J. Hudson, ed., *Australia in World Affairs, 1971–75* (Sydney: George Allen & Unwin, 1980), pp. 271–282.

Woodard, Garry, 'Relations Between Australia and the People's Republic of China: An Individual Perspective', *The Australian Journal of Chinese Affairs* 17 (Jan 1987), pp. 143–152.

Woodward, Bob (and Carl Bernstein), *The final days* (New York: Simon and Schuster, 1976).

Wurth, Bob, *Capturing Asia: An ABC Cameraman's Journey Through Momentous Events and Turbulent History* (Sydney: Harper Collins Publishers, 2010).

Index

Note: Page numbers in bold indicate photographs.